Blinded by Vision

The Secret Life of a Psychic

Written by

Tracy Williams,
Spiritual Consultant

With Nancy Figueiredo

Based on a true story.

BALBOA
PRESS
A DIVISION OF HAY HOUSE

Balboa Press books may be ordered through booksellers or by contacting:

Balboa Press
A Division of Hay House
1663 Liberty Drive
Bloomington, IN 47403
www.balboapress.com
1 (877) 407-4847

Printed in the United States of America.

ISBN: 978-1-4525-9026-4 (sc)
ISBN: 978-1-4525-9028-8 (hc)
ISBN: 978-1-4525-9027-1 (e)

Library of Congress Control Number: 2014900791

Balboa Press rev. date: 02/03/2014

Contents

Acknowledgements

This book would not be possible without Phyllis
C. Weber, AP/L.A.c. Acupuncture and
Energy Medicine

Those are her credentials, but I lovingly refer
to her as "Dr. Frankenstein." I would not be
alive today without her help. She has gone above
and beyond the call of duty to ensure my
good health.

To the angel who referred me to Phyllis, you
know who you are. Thank you.

To my two new angels, Linda Leith, Polarity
Loft and Dr. Jim Hogsed M.S.W., D.C
Thank you.

There have been many who offered their healing talents
along the way—to all of them, my gratitude.

To Linda Miller, for walking in when everybody else walked out.

Thank you to my friend Lauri, who put up with
me for many years, keeping me sane.

To Mary Ann, who has been dedicated to this project for over ten years. Thank you.

To Kim Allen, who never let me give up on the book.

To my family, both dead and alive, for their love and support. Thank you.

And of course, to Nancy, coauthor of this book, and one of my best friends.

Last, but certainly not least, all of my wonderful clients that have kept me in business over the years, all of whom have a piece of my heart.

This book would not be complete without the final blessing and editing of Renée Warthman. Thank you.

"Trust is the most valuable thing you will ever earn."
—Anonymous

Forward

"To one who has faith, no explanation is necessary.
To one without faith, no explanation is possible."
—St. Thomas Aquinas

We have all been faced with challenging situations in our lives. In those moments it would be so simple if a large book of answers would just fall from the heavens with solutions to all of our problems. That would be too easy, impractical, and a little dangerous—rain today with chance of a concussion.

I suspect challenges are par for the course. There is no easy way around lessons that need to be learned. We may not have that heavenly book but we do have Tracy. She is able to help us navigate life's unpredictable yet wondrous journey. Her insights are like markers on our own unique life map offering direction.

How we weather our challenges will define the very essence of our human experience. We are one but part of the all.

Introduction

Who is Tracy Williams and why would you want to hear my story? I was a normal girl, growing up in Queens, New York. Normal based on appearances but deep inside there was a psychic evolving, waiting to burst out. Let me begin by saying my psychic gift was inherited from my paternal grandmother.

My grandmother first met my grandfather when she was working as his employee for a garage door company. She was his secretary. Her skills were unmatched in typing, stenography, and overall office management.

Even though I inherited her amazing psychic ability, I did not inherit her secretarial skills. Because of this, I have a running joke with my clients. When I make mistakes I tell them, "I am a great psychic, but a horrible secretary." My errors are usually a result of scheduling appointments rather than psychic ability. For example, I have clients around the world and have to make sure I account for the correct time difference. This is why Nancy Figueiredo entered the picture, because I cannot put together a simple sentence or type very well, she graciously agreed to put my unusual story down on paper. I should also mention another one of my big dilemmas, I have extremely poor eyesight and some may even consider me legally blind. But I can see things other people can't, and have never missed having perfect sight. Even with corrective lenses, I have trouble reading and writing. I usually need the aid of a strong magnifying glass or a dear friend.

My grandmother was born wealthy, but struggled later in life. She had a civil servant job as a secretary, before becoming a well-known psychic. Her pseudonym was Celia McBride. She was married to my grandfather, a devout Catholic, for thirty-seven years. And from my understanding, they were thirty-seven pretty bad years. I guess you can say that I did learn from her mistakes and jumped ship. She died married to my grandfather and I did not want to follow the same path. I only had twelve bad years. More about that later.

People ask me, what is it like to be psychic? My answer is, "I don't know what it is to not be. It is all I have ever known." It is the same as someone who is tall, black, or Chinese. How can you know how to be anything other than what you are? Like anything else, you make the best of what you have to work with, and I am trying to be the best that I can be. Apparently, I have stepped on a lot of toes along the way but maybe that is due to my poor eyesight!

Once I went to the eye doctor to see if I qualified for laser surgery. One of the associates gave me the basic eye test with the letters on a wall, you know a big "A", a big "E", and they get smaller as they go down. I took my time taking the test and when I could barely make out the letter I would use my psychic ability and some deductive reasoning to fill in the gaps. For example if there was an "A", I knew that there would not be another "A" for a while. Even though it was difficult, I got every letter right. So the other associate took me in the back to dilate my pupils and give me a test where I had to look into a machine. I got nothing. I could only see black. I told him that his machine was broken. They asked me to wait back in the first exam room and I could hear them arguing behind me. The first associate said, "She can see, she got every letter right." The second guy said, "No she is blind, she thought the machine was broken." The banter back and forth lasted about five minutes, and then they both came into the room and asked me politely to please leave.

I lost my memory around twenty-seven when I had a near-death experience. I was basically born again into a new life, where I found myself married with two small children. But there was a minor problem; I did not remember who my husband and children were. The mind is an amazing machine, when something is buried, it will always resurface. It is like the desert, "nothing is ever lost." Even if it is buried deeply, the winds of time will expose it. I have spent the past twenty years, not only living my present life, but piecing back the fragments of a life that I once knew. It is extremely painful for me to remember some of the memories, so it is easier to pretend the old me was actually someone else. We will discuss my near-death experience in a later chapter because this was a pivotal time and the start of a new life for me.

The story you are about to read is unique, difficult to hear, and astounding. You are left to draw your own conclusions at the end of the book.

The events that occur through chapter six are from the life that was known to me before my near-death experience. It has taken me many years to piece together that life, through the aid of hypnosis, acupuncture, and self-therapy. Even though I remember the events that took place, I have learned to not allow myself to feel the emotions associated with those experiences, because it is unhealthy for me. When remembering my previous life's events I would get very sick. It was like feeling the pain of those moments over and over again. They were difficult enough the first time around and I have no desire to relive them again.

I refer to that time as my previous life because after my near-death experience I came back as someone else. Any one of the traumatic events I have lived through would be enough for the average person to endure in one lifetime. But the angels had to put in extra effort to catch my attention, prove to me I was psychic, and make me realize there was a different purpose for me. By virtue of being born under the astrological sign of Taurus I am stubborn by nature. The angels really worked hard to give me a wake-up call. It has taken me forty years to wake up.

I used to think I was unlucky because of the negative chain of events that have affected my life but, as my grandmother told me, I have become stronger because of them. Today I look back and see blessings. I feel they were necessary to help me evolve into the woman that I am today and for that I am grateful. I feel like I am the luckiest person alive.

Chapter One

What is a Reading?

Where do I begin? Readings have been going on for centuries. There have been prophets, seers, witches, oracles, shamans, and on the negative side; soothsayers and gypsies. Regardless of what they are called, all good readers will come up with the same answer, and this is one of the things I can take pride in.

Many of my clients have tried new psychics. Once I get past the jealousy, because I am human, I am amazed that some of the readers say exactly what I say. It is mind blowing to think the stuff that I tell people is being communicated, or rather downloaded, into my conscious thoughts by a higher power, it is even mover baffling to know that another human being is receiving this same data. On a grander scale, there are quite a number of psychics out there relaying the same information. I find this to be extraordinary, and I *am* a psychic!

I have such a loyal following of clients. Even though they may try other talent from time to time, in the end they always return to me. The reason for this, as I have been told by so many of them, is that, together, we establish a bond that goes beyond client and psychic. The result is that I truly care about my clients. I am rewarded by their satisfaction and happiness. Another reason for their loyalty is they tell me I have "laser beam accuracy." When I describe a picture, it literally comes true. If I were given a name of a person, I can describe that person's feelings, emotions, intentions, and physical appearance. Most of the time a first name is sufficient, but as we have learned from our own experiences, we often know more than one Joe, Mark or Mary. More information, like a last name or age, is sometimes helpful to differentiate between various people.

During my first reading with an individual I prefer to know as little as possible. I often just know them by their first name. Sometimes the readings are by phone and other times they are in person. When I read an individual in person, I sit them across from me, about a foot away. I have never actually measured the physical distance but there is a certain distance I innately sense to be perfect and arrange the chairs accordingly. Sometimes, to the irritation of my clients, I need to keep moving and adjusting the chairs until I sense the right energy, and only then can we begin.

Now we are ready for the reading to start. I hold crystals and rocks, each with their own special meaning. They help me ground my energies and offer me a calming point because I get very fidgety when I read. In my hands are pyrite, a ball of copper, and two pieces of coral from the ocean. In my lap I hold two quartz crystals, one from Peru, the other from Sedona, Arizona, and a raw, copper egg from the Congo, all gifts from clients.

I feel the Universe provided my clients, in their travels, with these gifts that in turn they gave to me, affording me the tools I need to read properly. Even though I have never personally travelled the world, I feel as if I have travelled it vicariously through my clients' own adventures.

The reading becomes like the "Perfect Storm" when all the elements come together. The sensation for me is like an energy vortex opening up in the midst of the reading. My body comes alive as if a surge of electricity is running through it. Visually, I feel as if I am in the middle of a 3-D movie of my client's life. I can see, feel, smell, and experience what they are feeling physically at the time of these particular visions. This connection can be problematic at times.

One of the reasons I do not like to do parties is that, more times than not, people are drinking. As the night progresses they generally become more inebriated and by the time I get to my last reading people can be fairly incapacitated. As their reader, I will get the sensation of their intoxication. For example, one girl was pretty buzzed as I proceeded to tell her that her father was going to have a heart attack. The entire time we were both giggling, she because of the alcohol she ingested, and me because of my psychic osmosis. The poor girl had a rude awakening as what was foretold came true, though she was not very aware at the time of the reading. She did not take my predictions to be true and did not fully retain the information she was given. Perhaps my own giggling did not help the matter either. But when her father had the heart attack she recalled what she had been told.

Experience has taught me to impose a two-drink limit from my clients at any of these parties. The only pharmaceutical drug that impedes my reading ability is "Zoloft." It is difficult, but not impossible, to read anyone under its influence.

If a client comes for a reading and is suffering with health issues, my body will mimic the symptoms that they are experiencing. For example, if the client has a heart condition I may experience chest pains. I have experienced everything from shortness of breath, headaches, leg pains, tremors, etc. These symptoms can linger up to a day or two after that particular reading. It makes it difficult to discern whether the pains are my own or if they are just sympathy pains I have inherited from the client.

The same is true with my personal thoughts. The wires get crossed a lot. I was dating a guy for about a year and on one romantic evening he was trying to get a little friendly. I kept telling him I saw four vials in front of me. I knew it had to do with an experiment, and I knew I had the answer but could not figure it out. I asked him if it was in his head, since he had a medical background, but he had only one thing on his mind.

The next day I had a reading with a scientist. She had a dilemma with four vials and she did not know the answer, but together we could figure it out. She was the reason I kept dreaming of the four vials. The moment she thought about calling me I was able to pick up on what was in her thoughts, in this case the four vials. This is the type of connection that I develop with my clients.

Sometimes readings are not what they seem. I have a client named Sandy, who I recently read. When we were talking about her ex-boyfriend I said, "You will be on his mind continuously, because he will see your name in print and all over the television."

"What could I possibly do to have my name everywhere?"

I replied, "I don't know, I just see your name in print and on TV."

About six months later, Hurricane Sandy devastated the Northeastern seaboard, and a couple of months after that there was a horrific shooting at Sandy Hook Elementary School. I do not think we have heard the last of that name, unfortunately.

As for my client Sandy, she is the sweetest, most wonderful human being, and these tragedies have absolutely nothing to do with her, except to accomplish putting her name in print and on TV everywhere. That was my connection to these horrible events.

When the universe provides information, anything can become a trigger; a sight, a sound, a smell, a feeling. I lived on Long Island, on the south shore, but left in 1997 for Florida. I told everyone I was worried about the hurricane that will hit Long Island, but they just laughed at me and said, "You're moving to Florida!" Nothing like having fifteen years advance notice. This is one example of how time, in and of itself, is so irrelevant in the psychic realm.

My biggest complaints from clients have always been about the time frame of events occurring, never about the accuracy of the events foretold. Time is my greatest challenge. If I can learn to dance the dance of time, together we can become the next Fred and Ginger, creating new tomorrows.

The following is a testimonial from one of my clients.

December 18, 2012

To Whom it May Concern,

How does one begin to describe the depth of council Tracy provides through her readings as a spiritual consultant? It is impossible because the magnitude of knowledge and comfort gained from even one reading reveals itself over time.

I first called Tracy during a time when my oldest son struggled with his career. We had never met prior to this phone conversation nor did she have any knowledge of my family or me. Yet the insights she provided during that first call were as if she had known us all our lives. I sought Tracy's council because I felt conflicted. My husband felt strongly that our son, Michael, should give up his dream to live and work in Japan and find work closer to home in Chicago. I disagreed. However when the doors of opportunity kept shutting, and Michael began to become depressed, I worried that my advice to follow his dream was in fact bad parenting. Tracy confirmed what my spirit already knew. This was his path to follow and I was supposed to encourage him. She insisted that I not worry because his job opportunity would come from a place in New York. She also told me that he would not have to fly anywhere for the interview. None of this made sense. Michael doubted this news because the companies that hired English-speaking adults for this type of work were all based out of California or Toronto, and they all insisted on in-person interviews. Michael knew the process well as he has flown to several interviews in both locations.

Despite the disappointments that followed during the next five months, I kept thinking of Tracy's words and continued to encourage my son. We were thrilled when we learned that a prestigious, Los Angeles-based company was holding interviews in Chicago. However, when Michael received a confirmation e-mail requesting an in-person interview, he immediately called me. Michael told me that the e-mail address included "NY" and that the interviewer would be flying in from his office located in New York City. Not only did Michael land this job, they let him choose the branch location. This was significant because Michael had fallen in love with a Japanese woman four years earlier. They had kept in touch through Skype and visits, but Michael felt strongly she was "the one." Tracy had also confirmed this in that first conversation, even describing in detail the engagement ring he would select for her and their wedding décor. Time has proven what Tracy had already seen. She was spot on with the description of the ring, and as they plan their summer wedding, the pictures of the décor they have chosen is exactly as Tracy had described.

Since that time, Tracy has helped locate items Michael lost in Japan, each time describing in great detail the places where these items were located. She has also provided insight into his future work endeavors, which I'm sure will also come to fruition. She has also provided insight for my other son, Andrew, as he selected the university he is now attending. Andrew has confirmed that Tracy accurately described his classrooms, his professors, and even something more curious. She saw him performing on a stage. Again, none of this made sense as Andrew is very reserved and soft spoken with no stage experience. When Second City Comedy Troupe came to his campus, Andrew and his friends were inspired to try out for the university's improv team. Not only was Andrew good at improvisational comedy, he continues to perform with this team in Chicago. Improvisational comedy has become a favorite hobby for him, something no one, not even his family could have predicted. And yes, he performs on a stage.

Not only has Tracy provided insight and guidance for other aspects of my personal life, she has provided valuable information in my pursuit as a doctoral student. She has shared specific things about my dissertation process that could not be guessed, that seemed inconceivable at the time she spoke of them. Recently, she shared that there would be a female professor who would come forward, who would hear of my research and be very interested. She described how this professor looked, even describing her long hair. She spoke of this professor's research interests and told me that this professor would be an important part of this process because of the help she would provide. Since my research has not yet begun and I felt I knew everyone who was part of this department,

I could not imagine who this could possibly be. About ten days ago, as I said goodbye to my instructor on the last day of class, the instructor pulled me aside. She began to tell me about a professor in the department who had heard of my research topic and became excited because it reminded her of a book she just finished reading. As the instructor told me that this professor thought I should get this book, I knew right then I was having another "Tracy Moment." Sure enough, the instructor then went on to repeat what Tracy had said to me almost word for word. When I went home that evening, I "googled" the professor's name and there she was, long hair and all. The professor's home page also detailed the research interests Tracy mentioned.

This afternoon, I spoke on the phone with this professor for the first time. Though she couldn't recall exactly how she heard of my research topic, she was thrilled to speak with me. She then provided several research documents that provide validity for the specific research methodology I intend to use. Validity is an incredibly important aspect of the process and the information this professor provided is immensely helpful! Every detail Tracy described about this encounter happened. Once again, I have learned that those things which Tracy speaks of that seem impossible are simply events that have not yet occurred. But they do occur, often when you least expect it. Please know that Tracy's gift does not diminish the relationship I have with my God. If anything, her insights strengthen and renew my faith! Biblical scriptures tell us that God will not leave us and will send others to provide help and comfort in our hour of need. Tracy is definitely one of those people.

Tracy has become more than an advisor to us. She is considered a trusted friend. The wisdom she shares is so unselfishly given, and every moment spent listening to her provides a deeper sense of self. What Tracy does is truly a gift, and we are thankful she has chosen to give so much of herself and her time in order to share this gift with others.

Sincerely,
Ruth Meissen

Chapter Two

The Big Bang

"*Somewhere, something incredible
is waiting to be known.*"
–Carl Sagan

It all started with a big bang in Howard Beach, New York. Well it always starts with a big bang, and then roughly nine months later a baby is born.

The proud parents, Ann and Bill Williams, welcomed a bouncing baby girl into the world on May 11, 1965. They named her Tracy. Her brother Jack would arrive just over one year later on May 18, 1966. Apparently August was an especially good month in the Williams' household for procreation. Instead of "May flowers", it produced "May babies."

One hot summer's eve, when I was about three and a half and my brother was about two and a half, I decided to share some baby aspirin with my baby brother. That is the kind of girl that I am, I like to share the tasty treats. One for Jack, and one for me, until the bottle was almost empty. Instead of completely finishing the bottle, I decided to save a little for next time. At that point, my mother walked in and screamed at us.

"What are you two doing?" She called for my father, and they rushed us to the hospital. Together, my brother and I had our stomachs pumped. After that I think they threw out the remaining bottle of baby aspirin. Party poopers! This would be the first of many events when I believe I had more than just luck and good timing on my side.

Jack and Tracy

Let's face it, at three and a half years old I had no idea what I was doing, but psychically I knew when to stop. Once I reached the level of toxicity, I did not let my brother or myself ingest another aspirin. I love my brother, I would never put him in harm's way, I just wanted to have some fun.

My mother came in at just the right moment—that was not a coincidence. My parents, at this time, did not know I had inherited my grandmother's psychic ability, so they pumped our stomachs because they felt it was the right thing to do. Psychic ability is not just about me, or the person in front of me, it is about everyone in my world connecting. Like ripples on the surface of a pond, we are all connected, everyone affects every other human being.

Since a very early age I have experienced severe fevers. We are talking temperatures of 106°-107° Fahrenheit. These temperatures result in febrile seizures. During one of these bouts I ended up losing most of the vision in my left eye. On another occasion, I was no more than four years old with a fever and severe asthma. I was hitting the breaking point, which most people would call death. I stopped breathing. When I woke up I was in my mother's arms in the backseat of our family car. I was more awake and aware than I had ever been but my body felt paralyzed. I could not move or breathe but I did not feel scared. All of my senses were heighted. I could smell my parents' fear mingled with my mother's perfume as she held me.

My mother was screaming frantically at my father, "Billy she's turning blue, she's turning blue! I think she has stopped breathing again."

I could see the sweat beading on my dad's neck as he replied, "I am already breaking the speed limit, we will be there in less than five minutes."

He kept saying, "Hold on little girl, hold on little girl."

I remember wondering where we were going? How long did I have to hold on?

I recall every word spoken and my parents' facial expressions during that car ride. This was my first out-of-body experience and a glimpse of what psychic ability was like.

*Dear Reader, The beauty of an out-of-body experience is that you experience everything that life has to offer but you feel nothing, you do not suffer, there is no physical pain, and no emotions. You are watching your life as a **detached** bystander watching a movie.*

This experience was exciting, and what most people cannot imagine is that I would do anything to recreate it. I did not have to because my life would afford me multiple near-death experiences. These experiences became addicting to me. They allowed me to experience a heightened sense of awareness and I craved more of it. The sensation was magical. It was like peering into heaven's window and then running back to Earth, but I wanted another look, and another, and another.

My parents decided to tell me at the tender age of five, that my paternal grandmother was psychic. This revelation came after I started asking them about premonitions and they felt the need to explain what I was going through. My grandmother was about five foot three inches and a little round about her middle. She had three children, two girls and a boy, my father Bill.

I idolized my grandmother, not just because she was a psychic. We had much more in common. We were both about the same height, the shortest ones in the entire family. We both had the gift of gab. I had conversations with my grandmother as if I was talking with my best friend. During these moments there was no age difference between the two of us. We talked about everything from boys and family, to future events. My grandmother was a cool lady. Hopefully one of my grandchildren will say that about me.

On the other hand, my paternal grandfather was six foot two, an alcoholic, and extremely religious man. He believed all the money earned by his wife's psychic readings should go to the church. Ironically, her earnings sustained the household, even though he demanded she pay a third to the church because he felt that what she was doing was against God. I always wondered, as an adult, if this was my grandfather's way of paying penance for his many years of alcoholism, rather than my grandmother's psychic gifts. He died when I was very young, and was unable to learn the truth.

My father was born in Howard Beach, Queens, New York. He had a very rough upbringing. Some may say he was a wild child. That is a trait I inherited from him. I am the life of the party and can tell a joke like no one else, just like my dad. I can also drink like one of the boys. I guess not all we inherit is necessarily good.

My father had jet-black hair. He was Welsh and French Canadian, with a hint of Italian. He was six feet tall with a heart of gold that melted when he met his wife. Despite his golden heart he also had occasion to step on a lot of toes throughout his life, another little trait I would inherit. I guess stepping on toes was a means of gaining someone's attention. Tact was a quality I would acquire later.

Needless to say, my father was my hero and my grandmother the heroine, in my life's movie.

I would later recall that, because of my grandfather, my father had a negative view of the church. I remember him saying, "The old lady (my grandmother) would work morning, noon, and night so that the old man could give it all to the church."

My dad had become embittered because his family had to go without to appease his father's altruistic ambitions. This also colored my father's opinions of psychics, which later affected how he viewed his own daughter. He had trouble accepting my gift because it did not help him rise above his financial situation. Unless I could find a way to make my father money, what good was my gift to him?

My family was always struggling month-to-month to make ends meet. This was the story of my childhood. The only time my father was interested in conversing about my psychic ability was if I had figured out a means of making the family more money. Later in life my father would come to realize the magnitude and value of my gifts, and it had nothing to do with money—it was priceless.

Not only was I the victim of my inherent psychic ability, but I became the center of an ongoing battle that would hold my family hostage from generation to generation. It was a battle between religion and alcoholism. The pendulum would swing between good, religion and evil, alcoholism, but not always so cut and dry. It is a strange, romantic pair. From grandfather to son, from grandmother to granddaughter, and the dance continues.

I knew from a very young age I was meant for other things but it would be a constant struggle for me to realize my life's path because I was always at odds with other people, especially my loved ones. When I was five years old, I was at a family barbecue when I had another brush with death.

My cousin Heidi, who was a good fifteen years my senior, was making a point and said, "You can put a baby in the water and it will instinctively know how to swim." A *baby*, not a five year old!

Not knowing I was to be her example, she threw me in the deep end of the pool. I began to gently fall to the bottom where I sat cross-legged, my short life flashing before me in a calm stillness. Oddly enough, I did not try to swim to the top. But that may have had more to do with the fact that I did not know how to swim. My father jumped into the water to rescue me, screaming, "She is not a baby!"

He brought me to the surface, gently rolled me on my side, and water came out of my mouth. When I came to, I looked over at my cousin and said, "I don't know how to swim."

Everybody just laughed. But this event lead me to have a deep fear of water that I am still trying to overcome.

Irony has a sense of humor because a few years later I would save Heidi's life, but that's another chapter.

It was a cold February morning in Howard Beach, New York. My very religious grandfather insisted that while living under his roof we go to church. So to appease him my mother was getting us dressed to go. As she was putting on our winter gear; hats, scarves, and gloves, I began to fight with her while she was trying to put on my gloves. I threw a tantrum.

"The dog is going to bite my hand!"

This was unusual for me because I was the good child. Even more unusual, we did not have a dog and that was my mother's argument. "There is no dog!" She said. "Put on your gloves and let's go."

As my mother pulled me outside, kicking and screaming, I dug my heels into the ground and tried to pull away. But I was no match for her. She was an adult and I was only five. In my left hand, I held a cookie I was eating and my mother was tightly gripping my right.

Within minutes of walking outside, I felt the cold air hit my face and the weight of a forty-pound dog as it lunged at me, biting my left hand! The dog wanted my cookie. I screamed with terror and pain. It all happened so fast. My mother pushed the white mutt away and began to tend to my hand. I stopped crying, looked my mother in the eyes and said emphatically, "I told you the dog was going to bite my hand."

It was my mother who now had fear in her eyes.

My mother was not very familiar with psychic abilities and only knew her father-in-law's contempt for it. This was an uncomfortable realization that she might have a daughter who was different. Whatever this was, she did not like it and hoped it was just an isolated incident. These thoughts my mother had toward my ability left me feeling very alone. I began to regard my gift as being something bad. I have struggled with these feelings most of my life.

Back at home, my father was concerned that if they did not find the dog that bit me I would have to endure shots for rabies. My father was an excellent storyteller and as he embellished, with gory details, the series of shots I would need injected into my stomach I became paralyzed with fear. Thank God they found the dog!

Chapter Three

Michigan Madness

*"We live our lives forward into mystery, and we do so with
faith and courage, for that is the mandate of life itself."*
–Stuart A. Kaufman

My dad took a job for Dannon Yogurt in Michigan when I was six years old. This was going to be the fresh start my family needed. Life was relatively normal and uneventful until I was eleven years old and entering the sixth grade. I was a typical kid, wanting to be as popular as I could, but also wanting to explore my psychic abilities.

I told some of the kids in my class that if they told me their home address, I would be able to tell them what their bedrooms looked like. And so it would go, I was given an address and would begin a visual reading of their bedroom, describing the smallest details and saying things like, "Boy, you have a lot of pink in your room", "My god you're a slob", or "Wow, you're mother must clean your room because it is so neat."

The readings could not have been more accurate and the proof was in the surprised looks on my classmates' faces. They were amazed at what I was able to tell them, from the clothing strewn about the floor, to the posters on their walls. They became more and more excited, crowding around me, everyone wanting a reading.

This caught my teacher, Mr. Greenstein's, attention and he asked for a reading as well. When I accurately described his and his wife's separate bedrooms, he realized this was more than just a trick. My teacher suggested there were universities that could study my psychic brain and make sense of it. All I could think was the only way they could study my brain was by cutting into it. I was having none of that. I quickly covered my tracks by saying my father was a magician and he always said, "A good magician never reveals how a trick is done." After all, I just wanted to be popular. I never wanted a lobotomy.

Later that same year, my father's company was doing a promotional event that lead my family to travel back to New York. While we were there, I stayed at my cousin, Heidi's, house. My parents would eventually move back to New York, to a house around the corner from Heidi.

Heidi had three kids, two girls and a boy. She had a lot of really good junk food, every baby-sitter's dream. My own parents were health nuts so all I had to do was play with my cousins and I could eat all of the junk food I wanted.

As a child, I was always very responsible. I had an innate ability to know exactly what to do in an emergency situation. It was a Wednesday evening and I was talking with my cousin Heidi in the kitchen as she was preparing an authentic, German dinner. She told me she felt dizzy and needed to go to the bathroom, "Would you mind watching the stove?"

I heard her go into the bathroom, shortly followed by a loud thud. I removed the dinner from the burner, turned off the stove, and ran to the bathroom. I found Heidi face down on the floor, the bridge of her nose was bleeding. I woke her up and carried her into her bedroom.

Heidi told me she couldn't breathe, that she wasn't feeling well. She felt warm, so I placed a cold compress on her head. Her doctor was a family friend so I called him and asked what type of medication Heidi was on. He told me to call 911 and gave me all of her information.

When the ambulance arrived, I told them that Heidi was in the upstairs bedroom. In the meantime, I told my three young cousins we were going to play a game of hide-and-seek. To distract my cousins while the paramedics were helping Heidi into the ambulance, I pretended to fall down the stairs so my cousins would find me, which they inevitably did shouting, "We found you, we found you!"

We played hide-and-seek for a couple of hours. They never once suspected their mother was sick. While in the hospital, Heidi was diagnosed with an ectopic pregnancy. It is not an uncommon condition, one in every 100-150 pregnancies result in this, but if I was not there to help, Heidi may have died.

A couple of days later, while we were still on vacation, Heidi was back home from the hospital but still not feeling well so I helped her with the kids. Heidi was cooking another wonderful dinner, when she became sad and said, "I wish my husband [Dan] didn't work so much so that he could be home with us."

Innocently I looked up at my cousin and said, "Dan is not at work, he is at the home of his other wife and child."

I guess saving her life was not long appreciated. When I dropped this bomb Heidi just stared and wondered aloud, "How could you be so mean?"

"I thought this was something that everyone knew and just chose not to talk about," I replied truthfully.

Flash forward eleven years and everyone did know. Heidi realized I was just trying to help. In her defense, she was unaware of my unusual talent. At that young age, I did not understand what my psychic ability was all about and what I was truly capable of doing. I was under the impression all I knew, and anything that would pop into my head, was common knowledge to everyone. I did not understand that this was part of what my gift entailed.

One saving grace of youth is innocence. I was unaware that I was any different. I knew my grandmother was psychic, but I did not know the full implications of what the word meant, and frankly, my parents were not about to tell me. I was left to discover the full range of my talent on my own. In the meantime, I began to treat the voices in my head as my own personal *Jim*iny Cricket.

As a child, when I watched the movie *Pinocchio* I remember relating to the character of Jiminy Cricket, Pinocchio's conscience, rather than Pinocchio. I felt perhaps my conscience was real, but unlike Pinocchio's, it did not have a name or assume the form of a cricket. I also believed everyone must have one of their own, one they could talk and ask questions to when problems arose.

I began to realize that my conscience was, in fact, my first guide. I had become familiar with him but only knew him by his voice.

I never saw him. It was a male voice that would tell me what to do, "Run!" or "Hide!" It would always protect me. I wasn't hearing with my ears, it was in my head. Although I never heard the voice out loud I could differentiate, by the tone that he would use, whether his commands were in whispers or screams. As I became more accustomed to communicating with my thoughts rather than words, I began to navigate the world using all of my senses.

Dear Reader, The beauty of this is that I am not even aware it is happening. It has become second nature.

Back in Michigan, I was home from school and my cousin Delilah, two years older than me, was spending her summer vacation with my family.

It was eleven o'clock one evening. Delilah and I were laying next to each other in my twin bed when we simultaneously announced we were having a strange dream. We were not quite asleep, nor were we really awake. In a trance-like state we both started talking about an ornate, antique key. The key was being placed into a keyhole and it began to slowly turn. The door gradually opened, revealing behind it a bright light. Our two hearts were racing in time with one another, anticipating what was on the other side of this mysterious door. We were sharing a premonition.

A loud noise outside the bedroom window caused us to wake up abruptly. With our last ounce of courage, we walked over to the window to investigate. Looking outside we saw opposite scenes. Delilah saw a big oval ship with lots of colorful lights, consuming the entire backyard—and I had a big backyard. I, on the other hand, saw a small round object with white lights. We both ran into my parents' room screaming. My parents discounted us as idiots and told us to go back to bed. Delilah never visited us again, nor have we ever spoken about what happened that night.

Summer was over, and school was back in session. It was a Friday night, and I had the whole weekend to look forward to.

At the time we were living in a tri-level house. The bedrooms were upstairs, except for my paternal grandmother's bedroom, which was on the main floor. The kitchen and living room were on the main floor as well. There was also a basement. It was my favorite home.

We had dog named Heidi, no insult was meant toward my cousin, we just liked the name. She was a black and white German Shepherd, which was rather unusual—go figure. Heidi was the sweetest, most well behaved dog. She could go outside without a leash, and never leave the property. Heidi would sleep in the hallway between my room and my parents' room, occasionally wandering in to check on my brother Jack. She was a great watchdog.

It was late one evening, around midnight, and I was trying to wake from a bad nightmare. Leaving behind the terrible dream, I felt like I was waking up in a more terrifying reality. Something was on top of me. This unknown intruder was large and heavy. I began thrashing around in bed trying to get out from under the weight that was pressing me into the mattress, my mind struggling to comprehend what was happening. Attempting to free myself from its grip, I finally managed to roll onto my stomach and closed my eyes in fear. I started to scream, "Leave me alone!"

My screams woke Heidi and she began to bark, waking the family. My parents came running into my room and turned on the light to find me shaking and in tears.

By this point I was hysterical, screaming that a monster had attacked me. "It was probably just the dog," my father said, attempting to calm me.

Heidi was sitting innocently in the doorway, just as confused as everyone else. But I was insistent. "Daddy," I said. "It wasn't Heidi, it was something bad."

I saw doubt in their eyes; maybe they thought these marks were self-inflicted. My parents proceeded to inspect my body and found deep scratches all over my arms and legs. But the most upsetting were the ones that went straight down my back. The scratches were deep and bloody. They did not look like anything made by a dog and the location proved I could not have done this to myself.

And that is when I saw the fear in my parents' eyes. It was the same fear I remembered seeing in my mother's eyes when she realized that I could be psychic.

Dear Reader, To this day no one knows what attacked me. I can only speculate that it was a demon but I have no idea why it would have singled me out. This experience contributed to my fear that I, with my gift, could be bad.

Our dog, Heidi

A few weeks later when I thought, "this too shall pass" (my family motto, we never spoke about things, but just pushed forward waiting for life to move on) I was again awakened in the middle of the night. This time it was the raised voices of my parents fighting with my grandmother that roused me from sleep.

My head clouded with sleep, I got up and walked down the hall to see what was happening. Bleary eyed, I sat on the stairs and asked, "What's going on?"

My mother was in tears and my father was in a state of rage. My grandmother was also there, her bags packed and preparing to leave the house. When she looked at me, her expression scared me to death. In my father's hands were crumpled up pieces of paper.

I looked at him, "Daddy, what are those?"

My mother begged him not to show me. My father turned angrily to my mother as he replied, "She may as well fucking know!" He handed me the balled up pieces of paper.

I put on my glasses and proceeded to read through them. My grandmother had scribbled things such as; *she is the devil, don't let her live, don't let her reach the age of thirteen,* and *somebody has to kill her.* I had already been struggling with the idea of good and evil but the events of this night intensified my internal battle. This was my grandmother, whom I loved more than anything in the world, betraying me. She was supporting my fear that I could be evil.

My grandmother left Michigan shortly after that and went to live with my aunt Barbara in California. She had not been gone very long when we learned my grandmother had colon cancer. She would survive, make a complete recovery, and have no recollection of that horrible night back in Michigan.

Life slowly returned back to normal, and we were heading into another summer. I was twelve. I met a new friend named Sherry at school. She came from a very wealthy family; her parents owned a large house in the middle of nowhere, or at least that is how it appeared. It was a long walk but in Michigan there was a lot of walking.

Sherry and I decided to have a fun-filled sunbathing afternoon at her place. Although the rest of the house was finished, the pool was under construction. They still had to pour the cement. After about three hours of baking in the sun, we decided to go into the basement, take a shower, and change into our pajamas.

Sherry was in the shower and I was sitting in a chair in the other room, waiting my turn. I was tuning a radio, when I felt someone behind me. As I was about to turn around, a gloved hand came into view and grabbed my mouth. I pushed away roughly and watched the figure of man clad all in black run up the basement stairs. I screamed in fear.

Sherry's father came running down to the basement while Sherry made her way out of the shower. I told them both about the man dressed in black that attacked me. Again, I recognized that look of fear in her father's eyes. He said there was no way the man could have gotten past him because he was in the kitchen, just at the top of the stairs.

Sherry's father grabbed both our hands and said, "I have to tell you kids a story. This house was already built when we bought it and there was a rumor that a little girl was murdered here, by a man dressed in black. He had thrown her lifeless body into the unfinished pool."

Holding my hand more tightly he said, "I heard that man was caught and killed. I thought that it was a rumor, but now I think you saw his ghost."

The next summer, I decided to visit my aunt Barbara and grandmother in California. I was thirteen. I remember being a little apprehensive about seeing my grandmother again, but everyone assured me she had no memory of the unfortunate incident, and she truly loved me—after all, I was her favorite.

From the ages of twelve to thirteen, I was a bit of a tomboy and ugly duckling. So my aunts Barbara and Lydia staged an intervention, and decided to give me a makeover. Aunt Barbara put me on a diet, and Aunt Lydia wanted to send me to modeling school.

What was supposed to be a peaceful vacation in California turned out to be the weirdest experience of my short life. Aunt Barbara was extremely strict. She had the six weeks of my visit mapped out to the minutest detail. On one particular day, she had my three meals planned out along with a visit to my uncle's office and later the beach.

After I finished my morning coffee I headed off to the bathroom. My aunt announced that she had a quick errand to run. She had to take a friend, who had hurt her foot, to the doctor. When she returned we could begin our day. While in the bathroom doing my business I went off into a dream state. I had an amazing premonition of my aunt stopping by her friend's house at the top of a hill. Her friend, with her foot all bandaged up, was making her way down the stairs. She was the lady in red; red lips, red clothes, red hat, red purse, red from top to bottom—what a vision.

Then my brain shifted and I was in an office. I could see a desk, a bookshelf, and a plant. I shook it off and said to myself, "What a stupid daydream."

I took a shower, got dressed, and waited for my aunt. In the meantime, my grandmother and I had a nice discussion. I asked my grandmother to read me, particularly because I wanted to know when I would meet a boy. After all, I was thirteen. My grandmother replied, "It will be today at the beach, his name is Steve. He will make a comment about your white bikini."

At that point Aunt Barbara walked in the door. "Are you ready to go?" She asked.

I told her I had a strange daydream, and began to describe in detail the lady in red, and the office I had seen in my vision.

My aunt's jaw dropped. This time, instead of fear, I saw excitement in her eyes. She verified my story, mentioning how hideous her friend looked dressed up all in red. She went on to tell me there was no point in going to my uncle's office because I described it perfectly. She turned to me and said, "Put your bikini on, and let's go to the beach!"

It was the most gorgeous day to go to the beach. I was standing in knee-deep water, while Aunt Barbara was sitting on her little beach chair reading her book. A handsome guy with brown, curly hair, walked over to me and said, "I noticed your sexy, white bikini. Hi, my name is Steve."

I screamed in his face and ran. I told Aunt Barbara that I was ready to go home.

It was one thing when I was relaying a premonition, but something completely different to be on the receiving end of one. I was freaked out. Aunt Barbara found it amusing that my grandmother's prediction came true so quickly and just laughed.

Tracy in her white bikini

Once I returned home to Michigan, my father received the news that I was a full-blown psychic. He came up with the great idea to take me to the dog track.

"The little girl is going to make us rich," he would say.

I would sit there at the track hoping to make my father's dreams come true. I told my dad, "Let's do a couple of practice ones first." After I successfully predicted the winning dog in five consecutive races my father decided it was time to make some money. I felt the dollars in his hand was all the money my family had to pay the bills. I turned to him and said, "Don't bet all the money."

My father must have heard the doubt and fear in my voice because he chose not to bet that race. The dog came in dead last. He looked at me and screamed, "What happened?"

I said, "I didn't want you to lose all the money."

The next three races, every time my dad went to the window, I gave him a sad puppy-eyed look and shook my head no. Each one of those dogs came in dead last. If my dad was going to place money on the race, I couldn't take the pressure of picking the winner, knowing what was at stake for my family.

Dear Reader, He never made a dime off of my talent.

At the age of sixteen, my family had already relocated back to New York. I was still suffering from the high fevers. This one fever was particularly bad. It was a few weeks before Christmas and I was staying at my cousin Delilah's house. My mother, her sister Tia, and her daughter Delilah, were all taking shifts watching over me.

The fever got so bad that at one point they placed me in the bathtub. I was unconscious, defecating and vomiting at the same time. My parents had no health insurance so it was up to them to keep me clean and alive.

During the course of my illness, I was experiencing what I refer to as the "Willy Wonka effect." I was floating down a chocolate river, took a rest at a butter cream iceberg, and landed on a potato chip beach. Of course I was eating my way through the entire journey. I was in heaven. "Look over there, it's a cupcake mountain! I am going to eat my way to the top."

While I was on my happy food vacation in reality I was starving to death. When I woke up from the fever I had lost thirty pounds in three weeks. And while I was thrilled with my new body, my family was exhausted. But for me it was the most delightful vacation I had ever been on. Imagine eating until your heart's content and not gaining a pound!

I was working with my mother at Aunt Tia and Uncle Wolfgang's bakery because my father had become disabled after a heart attack he had while we were living in Michigan. It was up to the Williams' women to maintain the household. It was my father's belief that women should just get married and have babies, never aspiring to anything greater. That was for the men to accomplish. My brother Jack was expected to be the one to pursue a future, go to college and become a professional football player.

If I was the base or pedestal, Jack was the statue that rested on it. Later on, in his first year of college, Jack tore his rotator cuff and his dreams of pursuing a football career were over. Funny how life always seems to throw you those curve balls.

Back at the bakery, I was very tired from lack of sleep. I was overwhelmed with nightmares of my grandmother dying. I would wake in the middle of the night to a vision of my grandmother's face, colored with putrid green and black hues. I kept begging my parents to call Aunt Barbara to see if she was okay. Aunt Barbara, for her part, did not want to worry us and kept assuring us she was fine. This went on for about two weeks.

One day at work my mother was extremely cold to me. I thought she was losing patience with my being up all night and being tired all day at work (and, by the way, still going to high school). By the end of the day my mother finally pulled me aside.

"I have to talk to you," she said. "Your grandmother died last night of a heart attack."

I did not shed a tear because I had cried every night for the last two weeks and nobody believed me. I felt that a torch had been passed from my grandmother to myself. It was up to me to maintain the psychic connection. I would miss her deeply, but little did I know she was not going very far, just the realm next door.

Aunt Barbara had packed up a few of my grandmother's belongings, clothes and shoes, and sent them to me since we wore the same size. My most prized possession would be inheriting my grandmother's crystal ball. Which, to this day, resides in my reading room.

27

Being seventeen, I would probably wear her nighties to bed, but I couldn't really work the rest of her clothes and shoes into my wardrobe. It was a real generation gap, fashionably speaking.

That night, as I wore one of her cuter nighties to bed, I was thinking about how much I had loved her. I started to feel arms wrapping themselves around me and squeezing. I became very upset and started to cry.

I heard a voice telling me, "Tracy, I just wanted to say goodbye and that I love you."

My grandmother's smell was so intense all I could think was that my aunt did not wash these clothes before shipping them to me. I ran out of my room and down the stairs, scared out of my mind.

I bumped right into my dad who was walking around downstairs, an unusual thing for him to do during the night.

"What's the matter little girl?" he asked.

"Grandma was just in my room, she hugged and kissed me goodbye."

My father started to cry and said, "She was just in mine too." He hugged me like he never hugged me before. Grandma had come and said goodbye to both of us that night. I thought for sure I would die of a heart attack. It has taken me a lifetime to get used to ghosts, that is to say, if one can ever really get used to them.

Dear Reader, Psychic ability encompasses all of the usual five senses; sight, sound, touch, taste and smell. There is also another sense, psychic phenomenon, which is why it is referred to as the sixth sense. Usually, when a spirit appears, they can use one to three of the senses, but never all five. My grandmother allowed me to experience her presence through my senses of smell, sound, and touch. I was able to smell her, hear her voice, and feel her arms around me. Spirit chooses what they want us to experience, and not the other way around.

Chapter Four

College Bound

"It is better to light the candle than to curse the darkness."
—Eleanor Roosevelt

I just turned 18 and there was only a month left of high school, when I started dating a boy named Scott. I really wanted to look good for my new boyfriend and my upcoming graduation day. A new artificial sweetener had just hit the market; zero calories, tasted just like sugar, and found in many "diet" products. In my effort to loose a few pounds, I had the brilliant idea to drink cans of diet Dr Pepper® for three weeks straight as my only source of nourishment. At the beginning, it seemed like a good plan but I would quickly learn I was allergic to this new sugar substitute.

I was at Scott's house, enjoying our date, when all of a sudden I fell to the ground, unable to move. I had no sense of direction. I could not distinguish between up and down, left or right. My head was stuck to the floor as if my ear were magnetically attracted to it. Scott was trying to pull me away with little success. He called my mom and told her something was obviously wrong with me. When the sensation wore off and I was able to get up, he took me to the hospital where we met my mom.

At the hospital, doctors examined me and found nothing wrong. I was beginning to feel better so they sent me home. Walking out of the hospital, supported by Scott and my mom, I felt the magnetic pull again and fell to the ground, my head inevitably attracted to the floor. Having no explanation, the doctors suggested I was making it all up and simply acting. My mom was angry at their "diagnosis" and took me home, frustrated with the entire medical profession.

After that day, Mom refused to buy any diet soda, believing it was the source of my illness. Naturally I fought her on this decision because I, like many teenage girls, was afraid of getting fat. However, once the sweetener was absent from my diet my symptoms improved. Perhaps it was the chemical reacting with my psychic brain.

I never did make it to my graduation but it was because of a completely different set of circumstances. I came down with a severe case of strep throat and was, again, besieged by high fevers. I was becoming more fearful of not feeling well, so I decided to crawl into bed with my mother for comfort. My fever was so high but I felt as if I were freezing to death. I begged her to hold me to make me warm. I began to feel like I was slipping into a warm blanket. I became unaware of my mother and, instead, saw my grandmother.

I was in a big, empty room and she was in front of me. I wrapped my arms around her and gave her a big kiss. She reciprocated. I began to notice my toes felt as if they were stuck in cement. I was unable to pull myself between that line of life and death. I knew I could not stay with my grandmother and suddenly felt as if I were ripped back into my mother's arms.

I woke to my mother crying, "Breathe, breathe!" Between her tears, she told me that my lips had begun to turn blue and that I was no longer breathing. I looked up at her and smiled, "I saw grandma." I definitely put a few more gray hairs on my mother's head that day. Unsurprisingly, I did not make it to graduation that day and the school had to mail my diploma.

The summer before college my mission was to party my ass off, while still working three jobs. I was a shampoo girl at the local hair salon, a waitress at a catering hall, and a hostess at a restaurant. I deserved some fun. Conveniently, the drinking age at that time was eighteen.

A couple of my girlfriends and I decided to go into the city to party at a club called The Limelight. We arrived and bought our first round of drinks. They were extremely expensive for our budget. A while later, a not so attractive guy started to chat me up. He graciously agreed to buy me more drinks and proceeded to tell me that he was a photographer for movie stars. He asked me who my favorite movie star was. At the time it was an actor by the name of Joel Higgins, who co-starred in the TV series "Silver Spoons."

Well, it must have been my lucky day. This nice photographer informed me he had just finished a photo shoot with him and I could have the outtakes from the shoot if I didn't mind walking out to his car with him to get them.

The naive idiot that I was agreed to go. I was so excited to get my pictures. The photographer started to go downstairs and as I was placing my drink down on the bar, prepared to follow, a set of triplets appeared before me. They were wall to wall beautiful with long, curly black hair, bare-chested, and wearing long pants. They were adorned with headbands, a tribal band bangle on their left arms, and each carrying a spear. No— it wasn't Halloween or the Village people, just New York in the eighties.

In unison they yelled, "Get behind the bar and don't move until we tell you!"

I did as I was told and crouched down low behind the bar. I heard my girlfriends calling my name and when I looked up the triplets were gone. So was the photographer.

My friend said, "It's too expensive here, we're going home." I got home just before the eleven o'clock news. I sat down to watch alongside my dad. A segment came on about a murderer and rapist that was prowling the city. He had raped and murdered quite a few women and was still at large. They projected his picture onto the screen. I turned to my father and said, "Daddy, he was buying me drinks the whole night."

I told my dad the story of the events that had transpired at the club. He turned to me and said, "You're one lucky girl."

My guides were definitely on duty that night. The triplets that appeared and disappeared just as quickly were angels rather than human, sent to keep me safe. Thank God, because I was so naive. As I was coming to terms with the spirit world, I was unaware of the bad people in the physical world and it seemed that danger was lurking everywhere.

Summer was over and college was beginning. I met a girl named Stephanie, whose parents owned a bakery. We became very close and hung out together a lot. One weekend we decided to go skiing for the day. We skied our hearts out and built up a ravenous appetite. On the way home, we decided to hit the bakery for some munchies.

When we arrived at the bakery, Stephanie introduced me to one of the bakers named Lucien. She whispered in my ear, "He is about your age and single." I gave him a once over and said, "God no." Apparently his feelings were mutual.

The following summer rolled around, and Stephanie had asked me to join her on her friend's boat. Little did I know the friend she was referring to was Lucien. His body was tan, with beautiful highlights in his blond hair. This time I wanted Lucien, and bad. Once again, the feelings were mutual. I recalled my grandmother's reading, especially the part where she mentioned how I would meet my soul mate "in a large area" and "he would have blue eyes". Not too specific, but good enough for me.

Lucien and I continued to date throughout the entire summer. We spent a lot of time on the boat. He even taught me to water ski. I was already terrified of water after my near-drowning experience when I was five. I had a fear of water and to be water skiing was a big deal for me. Lucien thought this was funny. As I was trying to get up on my skis, picking up speed, Lucien would cut the engine, popping me into the air. I landed face down, with the skis on top of the water. I managed to undo the skis, and untangle myself from the towrope. My heart was pounding, by now but at least my head was back above water. I screamed out to Lucien, "Come back and get me, I'm scared."

As he was turning the boat around, I felt something huge and slimy brush up against me and push me in the stomach. I could tell by the force of the object that whatever it was, it was huge. My skin started to burn. I noticed blood in the water and then saw a fin moving away from me. Lucien arrived and started to pull me into the boat, he said, "The tow rope must have cut you." I had cuts to both my thighs and a deep scrape across my stomach. I was in shock and kept saying, "Shark, shark, shark."

Lucien wasn't convinced. He said repeatedly, "There are no sharks in the Long Island Sound."

That night when we got home and were all sitting around watching the five o'clock news, the highlight of the evening was a six hundred pound shark pulled out of the Long Island Sound. They mentioned it must have been sick to wander in that close to shore. I turned and looked at Lucien, "You said no sharks in the Sound, huh?" Still, no one wanted to believe me. The blood in the water that day was not only from the towrope. It was also from the shark rubbing against my stomach trying to get his next meal—me.

The relationship between Lucien and me was continuing to progress and grow stronger. We even began to do our shopping together. We went to the local TSS, equivalent of Wal-Mart, to get some necessities. We were on our way into the store, Lucien was walking ten feet in front of me, a bad habit he had, when all of a sudden I started to scream. He turned and asked, "What are you screaming about?"

I pointed up at the sky and there were what looked like a thousand birds directly overhead. It was like the entire sky had turned dark. "I don't know what you are screaming about," Lucien said to me. "They won't hurt you."

No sooner did he say that a flurry of bird poop came down like a meteor shower, landing on my head. From that height, the poop actually hurt on impact. I was covered but Lucien was clean. He could not stop laughing. He thought it was the funniest thing in the world until I asked, "Are you going to let me in your car?" And then it was not so funny. After buying a new pair of sweatpants and a sweatshirt, he made me walk to a motel down the street, where I was able to take a shower and wash my clothes.

They say bird poop is good luck. If that is the case, I won the lottery that day.

Lucien and I decided to go on a double date with another couple, our friends, Bob and Tory. We were planning on going to the New York Aquarium for the day. We had become good friends with them and often did many things together.

I knew I possessed some unusual abilities and, as was most often the case, strange things would happen between animals or other people and myself. I never hid my abilities from Lucien, but when we were married he suddenly hated what I did. I guess he forgot that part of the vow that said, "For better or for worse."

On this particular occasion we were admiring a large Beluga whale, its tank measuring thirty feet high and twenty feet wide. I placed my hand on the glass and thought how beautiful the whale was. I felt love for it and connected with the whale as if I could have been one in another life. The whale started to bang its body up against the glass, as if responding to my feelings. I saw this large object beginning to protrude from its body and the whale began banging harder into the glass. My next thought was, oh my god, it must be having a baby! Lucien screamed at me, bringing me back from the beautiful moment I felt I was witnessing, "You're turning the whale on, the poor thing has a hard on."

The next thing I knew, I was being asked to leave by the park official for over exciting their Beluga.

I graduated college and Lucien and I got engaged. I started working in the hotel business for a hotel called Viscount, at Kennedy airport. I worked the early shift, by early I mean I was at work by four in the morning. On my way there I had to pass a very dangerous part of Queens, a borough of New York City. This particular morning I caught every red light. While sitting in my Mercury Capri at one of these red lights, I heard a very long screeching noise and thought to myself, someone is going to get hit.

Well by now dear reader, you should not be surprised to know it was me who got hit from behind. Since I was wearing my seatbelt, I ended up with just a little whiplash but I knew the damage my car incurred was much worse. Someone needed to pay for it and it was not going to be me. I got out of my car and walked over to the car behind me and began to bang on the tinted window.

Suddenly I felt like I was in a scene from the movie Good Fellas, gone bad. All four of the car doors opened up at once, revealing four very large men. All I could think was, oh shit!

One of the guys grabbed my wrist and tried to pull me into the back seat of their car. My saving grace was the only karate class I had taken, while living in Michigan, that taught me how to break free of this particular hold. My senses went into over drive. I escaped, jumped in my car, and continued to work.

I immediately called the police. It turned out that these guys were running a scam. They would hit a car, strip it for its parts, and rape or murder whoever was driving. The police said I was extremely lucky.

I had five hundred dollars worth of damage to my car but it paled in comparison to escaping with my life. Once again, my angels were working overtime. I started to wonder, if I could ever stop being psychic, would these unusual events stop occurring in my life? At that moment I realized my guardian angels are like my invisible safety net, keeping me out of harm's way.

Chapter Five

Happily Ever After—Huh?

"I have learned silence from the talkative, toleration
from the intolerant, and kindness from the unkind;
yet, strange, I am ungrateful to those teachers."
—Kahlil Gibran

My grandmother would always say, after every one of my illnesses, the more a psychic suffers pain, the stronger they will be. My grandmother believed that so I just dealt with whatever came my way so I could become stronger. In retrospect, it almost made my illnesses worthwhile. Maybe this was my grandmother's way of trying to make lemonade from the lemons life had dealt me. But these cursed words have haunted me most of my life.

Lucien and I were planning our wedding. We planned for the ceremony to be held in the catering hall I worked at while in college. As luck would have it, they were running a promotion for a free wedding and the event was to be held on the following Saturday. I invited my mother, future mother-in-law, and her two daughters to the contest. The goal that day was for me to win the free wedding, especially because Lucien and myself would be paying half of all the expenses for the event. Remember, money was always tight for my family.

Lucien's older sister was constantly complaining about having to spend a Saturday at this win-a-wedding competition. What should have been one of the nicest days for me was beginning to feel like a day in hell. My stomach began to hurt and the tension was mounting because I did not want anyone to be unhappy. But it seemed everyone was.

I decided to make the best of it and enjoy the day. After all, I was trying to win a contest. My psychic ability started to kick in and I repeatedly heard in my head that Lucien's older sister was the winner of the "ultimate wedding package." I kept telling myself no and going as far as hitting my own head to knock the thought out of it, but the premonition just kept coming stronger and stronger. As the day wore on, they finally announced the winner and my greatest fear was realized. My premonition was right. Lucien's sister won, and she wasn't even engaged to anyone!

Dear Reader, It is not within my power to control a premonition. This story is proof of this. I would have had the contest turn out completely different. I predict what I see as it is given to me by my angels and/or guides. I am only the messenger.

Although I did not win the contest, Lucien and I went on to have a beautiful wedding. So in the end, it all worked out. Lucien's older sister was married a year later, and is still married.

Life was good in our first year of marriage. Lucien was still working in the bakery, and I was at the hotel. One evening in early December I was heading home from work, it was about an hour commute, when a cousin who had passed on a few years earlier appeared to me in my car. I had always loved Muchie, my German cousin. She was a beautiful and creative person. Muchie passed at the tender age of nineteen.

While her spirit appeared in my car, she mentioned that she missed Earth and wanted to come back. I said, "Perfect timing! I would love to have a baby."

Muchie replied, "That's what I was thinking, I am glad we are in agreement."

I suddenly became aware of my surrounding environment. The sky was the most beautiful, ethereal color of pink I could have ever imagined. The scene was made even more unusual because it was December in New York.

The next thing I recall, I was in my driveway, with no recollection of the drive home. I walked in the door and said, "I'm home."

Lucien had candles lit and dinner ready. He said, "Tonight is the night that we are going to make a baby."

"What happened to you today?" I asked. I related to Lucien the events that had transpired in my car. In my mind, it was no coincidence. It was destiny.

Well, that night we conceived. Coincidently, that night also happened to be Muchie's birthday. Not knowing the proper protocol, I telephoned my gynecologist the following morning to proudly tell her I was pregnant, going to have a girl, and that I would require her services.

"How far along are you?" The gynecologist asked.

"About twelve hours."

After a prolonged period of laughter the doctor replied, "If you are still pregnant in six weeks, I will be more than happy to help you."

Six weeks later I was moody and cranky. I begrudgingly made my appointment. I was still a bit upset with the doctor for not believing me when I had first called. The doctor did recall that I had mentioned to her I was having a girl. I got excited when she confirmed my pregnancy. She turned to me and jokingly asked, "Do you still think that you are having a girl?" My mood quickly turning south, I mumbled, "Yes."

Lucien began to tell me that after the baby was born he did not want me to do my "psychic stuff." He said, "Once you become a mother, no more witchcraft."

Dear Reader, Little did he know the journey to becoming a mother actually intensified my psychic abilities.

I had a very difficult first half of the pregnancy. We were worried that our first child would be born with Down syndrome or neurological problems. After several grueling tests, my doctor announced that not only was it a healthy baby, but it was indeed a girl. The second half of my pregnancy went smoothly, except for the alarming weight gain of 75 pounds.

I had thirty-six hours of hard labor. After the thirty-fifth hour mark the doctors decided to give me Pitocin to speed up my contractions. I was exhausted and they feared I would be unable to deliver the baby. Once they induced me, the pain was so severe I was screaming as if someone was cutting off my legs. They tried to give me morphine shots in my stomach because I was refusing to have an epidural. Stubborn me. I was fighting for a natural childbirth. They tried to roll me onto my left side, because they felt it would be easier for me to give birth in that position. That would be the first sign that something was really wrong. The moment they would roll me onto my side, I passed out.

If they rolled me onto my back I was in excruciating pain and if they rolled me onto my left side I passed out due to even more pain. Unbeknownst to anyone, I was shredding my own spleen. Finally, after thirty-six hours, my daughter Megan was born naturally. Megan was perfect, ten toes, ten fingers, a happy, healthy, baby.

While in recovery the nurses were pushing down on my stomach to get the residual blood out. I heard one nurse mention to the other, "She's a bleeder." That struck me as odd because I really wasn't. This was sign number two that something more was wrong. When I weighed myself at the hospital, I lost sixty pounds from giving birth. Everybody, including myself, thought this was odd. They offered that I must have had a lot of water weight. After three days in the hospital, I went home to take care of my new baby girl. I felt so horrible and weak. I started to wonder how any new mother could care for her child, feeling the way that I did. I tried to tap into my own condition psychically, to get a better read as to what was going on with me, but it is hard to read yourself, and even harder when emotions are involved.

I was so weak that I had decided to nurse Megan while in bed. I placed a teakettle on the stove to make myself a cup of coffee. While nursing my baby, I fell into a deep sleep. I was awoken by the sound of the fire alarm. Some how my kitchen curtains had caught on fire. I was able to put it out, but thought to myself, what is wrong with me?

The first thirteen months since delivering Megan, I felt constantly nauseous and tired. My symptoms became so severe, that I was rushed to the hospital with a high fever, caused by a very unusual inner/outer ear infection. I was on so many antibiotics that the doctors said I would have to stop nursing. As a strong advocate for breast-feeding, this made me extremely sad.

At the hospital, a nurse had seen me crying because my milk had finally dried up. To this day I am not sure if she was a nurse or an angel. She turned to me and said, "If you strongly believe that you want to nurse your baby, just let her suckle until your milk returns. It will hurt, but it will return."

She went on to tell me that in some third world countries if the mother died the male parent could make milk to feed the baby. Whether it was a true story or not, it served its purpose. It made me believe that I could once again nurse my own child. I did resume breast feeding my child and found out, via an internet search, that men can, in fact, breast feed as well. In certain cultures, in the event the mother dies, the father will be able to produce milk to feed his child.

My symptoms did not subside and I began to lose a lot of weight. I looked thin, although the scale said I weighed much more. Lucien and I had, in the meantime, bought a new home. Everything seemed very normal. We were getting a bigger house, our baby was growing beautifully, and we were hoping to have another baby. Money was tighter than it ever was and we really could not afford our new home, but we did it anyway.

I was extremely excited when we moved in. Within twenty-four hours, I had the house looking as if we had been there forever. My parents came to visit and noticed how poorly I was looking. They asked, "Are you eating, you look so thin?"

I told them, I still weighed one hundred forty pounds, but I was having trouble keeping food down, and difficulty breathing. Within days of their visit, I would bend over and throw up water.

My breathing became more labored, and my hair began to fall out. I went to the doctor and said I was going to give myself a tracheotomy because I couldn't breathe. I told my doctor I saw the procedure done on the television show "ER." Apparently I can use a pen to make the incision. My doctor laughed.

He said, "I can see that you are having trouble breathing, but why don't we start with a chest x-ray?"

And so my nightmare began. The x-ray revealed that a ten-pound cyst that was once my spleen was crushing my lungs. That was why I was having trouble breathing.

This discovery required emergency surgery. My mother Ann was, at this time, working in the bakery with Lucien. When she and Lucien were discussing my condition, Lucien got mad and said, "We can't afford a surgery because we just bought the house."

Lucien was becoming increasingly more and more angry at me for not stopping what he felt was something I could control. He stormed off.

In the bakery that day was a young woman who turned to Ann and said, "I couldn't help but to over hear your conversation. I happen to work for the top doctor in New York City, whose specialty is in splenectomies."

My mother put the young lady and myself in touch. I stressed to her how tight we were for money, and how my husband was against the surgery. She mentioned that she would speak with her doctor about having him just accept the insurance. She also offered to personally drive me to and from the hospital.

After the initial consultation with the surgeon, he was scheduling me for the weekend before Valentine's Day. I asked, "Can we make it the following week? In the bakery business, that is a very busy week." The surgeon gave me a stern look and added, "You're lucky if you make it that long." It seemed as if I was always facing death, like staring down the barrel of a loaded gun. I was scared and confused, and wondered, "How many lives do I really have in me, before my luck runs out?"

I went in as scheduled. As I was being prepped for surgery, they asked if I wanted to take anything to help calm me down. I told them, "No that won't be necessary. I had a long talk with my dead grandmother and she said I would get through this just fine." I was in the hospital all alone. My mother and Lucien were working at the bakery and the rest of the family was taking care of Megan.

While on the operating table, the surgeon said, "I am going to give you something that will make you feel a little sleepy." For me, the effects were the equivalent of being happily drunk. The surgeon began mapping out his cutting strategy, drawing on my stomach. All the while I kept saying things like, "Take pictures, cut as much as you want." I continued to talk up until the moment I was intubated. It was a seven-hour surgery. When they removed my spleen and went to place it on a scale to have it weighed, it burst. Talk about the nick of time.

In the recovery room they told me that my rib cage had been bent upward. It would feel as if I had twelve broken ribs. They decided to give me Demerol for my pain. The Demerol made me crazy. I thought that I was Superman, and could fly out my hotel window. I believed I was in a hotel on vacation—and feeling no pain. It took seven orderlies to get me back into bed. I was a strong little super hero but those orderlies were my kryptonite.

Once the Demerol wore off they decided to give me Morphine instead. That only made me extremely nauseous, and I threw up my guts. With the hundreds of stitches holding me together, this was not such a good idea. The surgeon said, "We have a problem. You react so badly to the various pain medications that we have tried to administer that I don't know what to give you." I replied, "Give me a Tylenol, and let me sleep it off." He agreed. Sleep has always been my answer to healing my many illnesses. They were quite amazed that I did not need any pain medicine.

Shortly after that, Lucien's best friend Mark was getting married. In my condition I would not be able to attend the ceremony because I was still in the hospital. So Mark paid me a visit and said, "I am sorry you won't be able to make it to the wedding. I hope that you get better soon."

I innocently replied, "Don't worry, I'll be at the next one." He looked a little perturbed. Too much information. Two years later, I did attend that one.

Dear Reader, With all the pain that I had just endured, my only thought was, I am going to be the best psychic ever, just like grandma had told me.

A year or so had gone by and Lucien wanted more children. My doctor advised against my getting pregnant because my immune system was so weak. Lucien and his family began to put a lot of pressure on me. I gave in and tried getting pregnant again. When I didn't get pregnant right away, we decided to get a dog instead. The dog was a half Shepherd, half chow mixture that we named Barney. Immediately after welcoming Barney into our family, I got pregnant.

Shortly after that, Megan came down with the chickenpox. I was only a few weeks pregnant and pretty sure I never had them. Being Megan's primary caregiver because Lucien worked so many hours I called the doctor, concerned for my unborn baby. The doctor said, "You probably just don't remember having the chickenpox, but there is a test that we can administer to see if you did."

By the time I received the test results confirming I never had the chickenpox, I already contracted them from Megan.

My case was so severe that I was covered head to toe with chickenpox, inside and out. Up my nose, in my ears, and of course I had the high fever to go with it. The only course of action was to sedate me so that I would remain unconscious. The good news is that I don't have any chickenpox scars, because I could not scratch. The bad news was that it was extremely dangerous for my unborn child. I had to undergo a battery of tests, one of which could have caused me to spontaneously abort. The doctors were adamant about giving it to me. I was seeing genetic specialists because they could not believe that such a young fetus, exposed to such an extreme case of chickenpox, could actually turn out normal.

They gave me six months to decide whether I wanted to keep the baby, while the testing continued. Lucien left the decision completely up to me. On the final day, I sat in Megan's room, and prayed to God. I said, "What do you want from me, am I to raise a physically challenged child?"

The room began to fill with the most beautiful, yellow glow. I felt warmth consume my body as if God himself was touching my soul. I heard a male voice, soothing and gentle, music to my ears. He said, "Have her, she will be perfect." And I thought to myself, "Oh, another girl." But once I decided to keep my baby, I couldn't find a doctor that would take on the risk of delivering her.

One of my friends referred me to a doctor she knew. This doctor told me that she would have no problem delivering my baby. I contracted strep throat close to my delivery date, which did not seem to worry my doctor at the time. I was in her office for a routine checkup, when she said, "The baby's head is crowning. You have to go to the hospital."

In the delivery waiting room of the hospital I made friends with another mother, Lily. Again, I was adamant about having a natural child birth and screamed so loud during the birthing process that Lily insisted on drugs for her own delivery, saying that she didn't want to end up like me.

I felt no pain in my stomach at all. Apparently my nerve endings were damaged from the splenectomy I had. I did have a ton of pain in my hips and knees, as odd as that may sound. I heard someone suggest that they give me Pitocin again, after only four hours. I was so afraid about getting the drug because of the overwhelming pain I endured the last time that I managed to speed up my own contractions. My baby arrived shortly thereafter.

Ten fingers, ten toes, she looked perfect to me. Not long after, while I was in the recovery room, they asked me to sign a waiver for a spinal tap for my newborn because she was extremely jaundiced. I only held her for a moment, she was too lethargic to nurse, and then they took her from me to do the procedure.

More bad news. The test confirmed that she had spinal meningitis. Ironically, it wasn't from the chickenpox, but the strep throat. It was one thing when bad things were happening to me, but it was the absolute worst feeling when they started to happen to my children. Every mother wants to take their child's pain away. It is a human instinct.

As my baby lay in ICU, with the other sick babies, I noticed Lily's baby was in there as well. Lily had given birth to a son. The umbilical cord had been wrapped around his neck and he had suffered oxygen deprivation. Lily's father was a minister, who happened to be visiting his newborn grandson in the ICU. I turned to him and demanded that he pray over my daughter, Marie, and his grandson, Conner.

He said, "Today I am here as a grandfather, not a Minister." I became angry and said, "You are always a minister, now pray!" I pointed my finger at him and I told him that the two newborns would get better, and be released on the same day. He prayed, and my prophecy was fulfilled. God had kept his promise to me.

Back home severely in debt because I owed the hospital about sixty thousand dollars for their share from my splenectomy, Lucien was relentless in telling me I needed to go back to work, so that I could pay off my medical bills. It made no sense for me to go back to work with two small children at home. By the time we paid for daycare, anything that I could possibly earn would be eaten up and I did not have kids for someone else to raise them. Besides all that, I still did not feel well.

Easter was a week away. Megan was almost three and half years old and Marie was about three months old. I was planning on having the whole family over and life was good again.

Chapter Six

He Said His Name Was Jimmy

*"If I'd paid attention to what others were
thinking, the heart in me would have died. But
I was much too stubborn to ever be governed
by enforced insanity. Someone had to reach for
the rising star, I guess it was up to me."*
—Bob Dylan

It was Good Friday morning. In preparation for the family get together on Sunday, I had all the cooking done and was about to start cleaning. I had two days to make the house look perfect. That is when my fever started. I began to feel nauseous and all I could think was, Oh no, not again.

As my symptoms progressed, I started vomiting and noticed there was blood. This was a new experience, even for me.

For the first time ever I was getting scared. I guess I was due to run out of luck sooner or later, despite those pesky birds pooping on me millions of times. This time things were different. Something felt very wrong and I could not shake this impending feeling of doom.

Where was my grandmother? Why wasn't she coming? I needed her to tell me everything was going to be all right. I gathered my girlfriends together to make sure my kids would be taken care of. I had the best group of friends. They assured me not to worry about the girls. My aunt Lydia arrived to take me to the hospital. As I kissed my babies goodbye, I thought it was going to be for the last time.

When I arrived at the hospital, my family doctor was there to meet me. They began to run tests. My doctor and I had become close over the years, by now he was more like family. I looked up at him and asked him to just give me some medicine and send me home.

And then I noticed the tears in his eyes. He took my hand with both of his and told me, "I don't think I can save you this time."

He explained to me that I had a staph infection in my blood and was going into septic shock. The infection was spreading too rapidly and he wasn't sure where it was coming from. He believed I would be dead in two hours.

Apparently, while I was breastfeeding my daughter Marie, I contracted an infection from her. Luckily, Marie was in no danger but the infection went into my blood stream, becoming systemic. This was compounded because I no longer had a spleen and my body was unable to fight off infection as efficiently. I felt that I had survived one battle but still had an entire war to fight, and I was loosing.

I was admitted at Mercy, a Catholic hospital, to an isolation unit where I would not "contaminate" anyone else. What a comforting feeling. Being Good Friday evening, it was not staffed as well due to the holiday. I was lying in bed, in so much pain it hurt to move. I was aware of every part of my body and it hurt, from my toenails, to my earlobes. Even my eyelashes felt as if they were branches carrying the weight of snow.

As the pain persisted, my fever felt like it was continuing to climb. When a body temperature is high enough, it is not uncommon to hallucinate. I began to slip in and out of consciousness.

The drastic way in which the infection took over my body did not leave anyone feeling too hopeful that I could ever recover. I was dimly aware, perhaps more psychically than consciously, of a nurse coming into my room to take blood. She picked up my arm and muttered to herself, "This one's a goner," before dropping my arm back onto the bed. "I'll come back and call it in the morning." And she walked out. She didn't draw my blood but drew her own conclusions instead. My eyes may have been closed but I knew how she looked. She had pale, white skin, long black hair, and was in her late fifties. I made a mental note of this and planned on reporting her if I got better.

I was aware of a candle at the foot of my bed and thought, being at a Catholic hospital, how nice, they lit a candle for me. I thought that was what they did when a person was dying.

Psychically I watched as the candle exploded into a gorgeous sun and the room filled with golden light. It was the same light I experienced when I heard the voice telling me my daughter Marie would be okay. It felt warm and comforting and filled the room with a loving glow. It was my own personal sun shinning down on me, courtesy of God. From that moment on I would always equate God with the sun.

The light began to pull me up. At the same time, its warmth and familiarity were caressing my body, removing the feelings of pain and discomfort that were previously consuming me. I was following the light to its source, not that I had a choice in the matter because it was drawing me in, but I was going willingly.

I found myself in a cave. I believe I was in heaven. It is my belief that heaven consists of only what we love and the beauty of those things will surround us. As a result, it will look different to each of us. I love caves. I have always found them comforting and enjoy their naturalness, their beauty. This cave was indescribably beautiful. I could hear the peaceful sound of a waterfall cascading down the walls. The cave felt alive, as if it had a presence of its own. The golden light that carried me from my room filled every inch.

I arrived in front of 13 beings standing around me in a semi-circle. They were wearing dark, hooded robes, reminiscent of Franciscan monks. Where their faces should have been I saw only darkness. These beings were unlike anything I had come across before, conscious or otherwise. They were wise, in possession of all knowledge known and unknown to man. They gave the impression they held the knowledge of the universe. And this cave, with its occupants, held more than just knowledge. It contained truth. It was as if every inch, even the air, was infused with this truth.

Later, I would make a connection between these 13 beings without faces and the thirteen crystal skulls. The crystal skulls are supposed to have come from 13 different planets and contain all the knowledge of the universe. They were brought to earth to the Atlanteans and can be seen in many different traditions. It is my belief that these 13 crystal skulls belong to these robed beings without faces. Leave it to me to bypass the skulls and go straight to the sources!

I had conversations with each of these 13 beings simultaneously, feeling 13 different emotions at once, and understanding each conversation as it was taking place. Talk about being able to multitask! I felt like a genius and thought this must be what it is like to be dead. It was as if these beings were uploading large amounts of information to me, giving me information about the past, people who had come before me, and the future.

During our conversations, I noticed a young woman approaching from my left. Her beauty was captivating, distracting. From an early age beauty was important to me and I had always wanted to look like that. The beings told me this was the true me, how God had created me, and how I would look if all the traumatizing events and illnesses had not happened to me. This knowledge was irritating. Taking a closer look, I realized she did resemble me and this was not what I wanted to see. I wanted to know how they, how God, could have let all those things happen. I wanted to be that girl. I did not understand why I was seeing this.

I asked the beings why they were showing me this? It was like a slap in the face, seeing what I could have been but am not because of all the things I felt I was forced to go through.

At that moment something even more unexpected occurred. The young woman that had been approaching walked up to me and then walked into me. I felt her become part of me.

And then the beings told me I needed to go back to earth, back to my hospital room. There were still things I needed to do. I argued but a voice, that I thought was God, was insistent. I wanted to obey that voice (although I felt like I couldn't not obey it) but I did not want to go back! Why would I want to leave this beautiful, loving place? Why would I want to leave heaven? I pleaded with the voice to reconsider returning me to such a terrible world. I thought of my girls and momentarily tried to convince myself they would be ok and would not miss me, after all, they were young. That brief, selfish, thought would continue to haunt me after this experience. I felt like a horrible mother. How could I do that to the two people I loved most on earth?

The next thing I knew, I was back in my bed at Mercy Hospital. So much for pleading my case. My first reactions were sadness and anger. I felt like I was kicked out of heaven. Not only was I feeling isolated on this earth dimension, alone in my room without visitors, but heaven did not want me either.

What I failed to realize at the time was that I was chosen to do a job. Later I would be able to see this experience as a gift and a new beginning. It would be the day I was reborn into the world. When I was returned to my hospital bed, I had forgotten everything in my life that lead to this moment. My life was a clean slate.

Dear Reader, Here I am, in my late twenties, no memory about how I got here and I had to re-learn everything. To this day, my own mother swears that I came back as someone else.

During the course of my experience in the cave and my conversations with the 13 hooded beings I believe they imparted to me all the information I would need to be the psychic I am today and to do the job I was chosen for. I believe the woman I saw in the cave was my higher self, and all that is good about me, joining me. I have never been as good as I am now, and I feel that I continue to improve everyday. My entire experience with the hooded beings felt as if it lasted six hours, though I concede it could have only been 6 minutes. I have no tangible proof. All I do know is that it happened within the length of time it took the nurse to return the following morning to make her call.

When the nurse walked in to my room, to her surprise, I was still very much alive, albeit miserable and in pain. I was confused and trying to make sense of what occurred. Was I hallucinating? Was I dying? Was I not dying?

It was Saturday morning and the sun was just about to make its way over the horizon when I heard a knock on the door. My visitor asked for permission to come in, he was interested in speaking with me. Thinking it was a doctor, I agreed. It was love at first sight. The man that walked into my room appeared to be in his seventies, with white hair and blue eyes. He was dressed in what looked like pajamas. I was captivated by his beauty. After my experience with the 13 hooded beings, I was still trying to determine what was real and this was becoming more difficult at every turn.

The man introduced himself to me as Jimmy. "Hi," I replied. "I'm Tracy." I explained to him that I was really sick and unable to shake his hand or touch him.

"Where are you coming from?" I asked.

He replied, "Three doors down with three other guys; Max, Ralph, and Bill. I am a patient here as well. I thought I'd keep you company."

He sat beside me and began talking. I didn't have the strength to entertain my new guest or attempt to hold a conversation so I was, for the most part, ignoring him. Suddenly he said to me, "Why aren't you listening to me?"

I was a little abrupt as I replied, "What part of sick aren't you understanding? I feel bad, I'm miserable, I have a fever, I'm freezing, and I can't get any blankets."

"If I get you blankets will you listen to me?" He asked calmly.

"It would help but good luck. It's a holiday weekend at a Catholic hospital. There's no one here to get them for you."

He stood up, his hands out in front of him and, speaking to the ceiling said, "God, I need blankets before finishing our job." All of a sudden "poof" there were blankets in his outstretched hands.

51

He moved toward my bed and carefully covered me with the blankets, never actually touching me himself. Was he an apparition? Real or not, the relief was instantaneous. Like magic, as soon as I was covered with the blankets my fever broke and I began to feel better. I had the strange sensation my mother was holding me. I was taken aback by how strong this feeling was.

Jimmy asked again, "Are you going to listen now?"

"Yes," I replied. "I'll listen now."

He began by asking me to recall an incident years prior, when my cousin threw me into the pool causing me to nearly drown. He explained to me that was a test to see who would help and who would not. My father passed. He proceeded to revisit every significant incident in my life. Each time he would tell me who passed, and who failed. Lucien's family failed each and every time.

Each one of my near death experiences had been tests for other people. God was using me as a means to test them.

I wasn't too hip on this idea, and inquired if they could find someone else. I felt rather offended by the entire situation.

Jimmy said, "No Tracy, it's you."

This was not an issue I could dispute, it just was.

Jimmy continued, "Don't worry, you'll be rewarded for your efforts."

I said with a sad and raspy voice, "You know, it's really not fair. I look awful. I've been cut up with surgery, and not to mention all of my crazy illnesses. I'd rather you just give me a break and use somebody else for a while."

Jimmy said, "When it's over, you'll be one hundred percent. You will be perfect and whole again."

I recalled the girl I saw in the cave. The one that was inside me, the one little by little I was becoming. It was weird, but physically I felt myself getting stronger. I believed that one day, the two would be one again, and that my body would be restored to perfect health.

Jimmy continued by saying, "I have a lot of work to do, because I have to finish what they started."

"What is going on here? You told me you were a patient, three doors down, and now you're telling me you have to finish what they started. Who the hell are you?" He replied, "You mean who the heaven am I?"

The whole world seemed to turn on end. Jimmy would spend the better part of that holiday weekend, Saturday night to Sunday morning, with me. He visited me a total of three times, before I was sent home on the morning of Easter Sunday.

While we were talking Saturday evening he said to me, "I miss my wife. I loved her more than anything in the whole world."

"Then go back to her. Where is she?"

In a sullen voice, Jimmy said, "I had to leave her. I had to go away on a trip I can never return from."

To which I added, "That's not true, you can always return. Even if it has been a long time, just go back, and she'll forgive you."

He insisted, "No, I can't but, I loved her more than life itself. We were separated by World War I."

I couldn't figure out how long ago that was. I didn't understand and kept insisting he could go to her and she would welcome him back. As it turned out, Jimmy had died in that war. He wasn't real in the sense of a physical presence, like you and me. He was an angel.

He began telling me all the things I had to do. He told me I needed to get started being a psychic and what I needed to do to accomplish that goal. He advised me to listen only to the voice in my head and to what the angels would tell me. He made me swear never to use tarot cards. And so, to this day, I don't use tarot cards.

At the end of the conversation, I agreed to comply.

He added, "If you listen to us, and you do what we tell you to, you will be rewarded." I feel this has been the case and they always have my back.

I was told so much information, some of which I cannot recall, but know it lies dormant, ready to be used when I need it.

Some of what I was told involved events that would occur in the future, or of people who came before me and failed. This was a lot of information, too much for the average person to comprehend without feeling overwhelmed and burdened. I was reassured that I would always have this kind voice to support me by saying things like, "Don't worry, don't worry. You're okay, you're okay, just let it in." Jimmy was like a mentor to me.

It was Easter Sunday, and if I may borrow a line from Dickens, "The spirits had managed to do it all in one night." I was feeling better and, as I stood in the doorway of my room, my doctor told me he was releasing me that day. I saw tears in his eyes again as he told me my recovery was nothing short of a miracle. "You have no idea." I told him one day I would tell him the story.

He went to get my paperwork. As I stood there waiting for his return, I saw Jimmy on the right side of the hall, coming toward me. He appeared to be floating rather than walking. I recalled thinking as I saw him approaching, "Oh my God, it's going to take him at least two hours to get to my room at this rate."

Trying to be polite I averted my gaze upward, but in the instant that it took for me to return my gaze toward him, he was right in front of me. It could not have been more than a minute later.

"What did you do, run? How did you get from there to here in the time it would take for me to snap my fingers?"

Jimmy simply said, "Look, I'm leaving, and you're leaving too." "How did you know that I was leaving?" I inquired.

As I continued to speak with him, he was gradually disappearing before my eyes. I moved to touch him and literally put one of my hands right through him. I gasped as I tried to understand all that was happening, and more importantly, who this Jimmy person really was.

Jimmy told me, "I have to go and I won't see you anymore. Not like this, but one day, we'll work together. You and I will work together and we will be together again."

Many thoughts ran through my head as I tried to figure out what Jimmy meant. I felt he might have been talking to me as one who had been a guide, and who would be again. In my heart, I felt that Jimmy meant I too would become a spirit guide, just as he was.

As it turned out, I would end up working with Jimmy for four years. He would be my guide.

In the instant that my hand swept through Jimmy, my doctor returned, literally walking through his disappearing figure. As he stopped in front of me, Jimmy was gone.

With a smile on my face, I thought, "I am not going to say anything, because if I do, my doctor won't let me go home." I was anxious to leave. Let's face it nobody likes hospitals.

The moment had arrived and the nurse came to collect me for discharge. As she was wheeling me out, she asked, "Did you say goodbye to your friend Jimmy?"

All I could think was, "These people are really fucking with me." Jimmy just disappeared in front of my face, and now this nurse is asking me if I said goodbye to him.

Playing along, I said, "Now would that be the man wearing the pajamas?" I didn't want to get into trouble for being crazy.

The nurse replied, "Yes."

For sanity's sake I tried to clarify, "The man who was three doors down, sharing the room with Max, Ralph, and Bill?"

To which the nurse replied, "No, no, no." Okay, so now I was thinking I was going crazy.

But the nurse continued and said, "Max, Ralph, and Bill were three doors down from your room, but Jimmy came up the elevator each and every time and went straight to your room."

I sighed in relief. I wasn't going insane. I did see him and those three guys were in the room down the hall. Jimmy had, in fact, told me the truth.

I returned home in time to feed seventeen people Easter dinner, only to collapse again. I had faithfully assumed my role as wife, mother, and maid, even after enduring the stressful weekend.

What I could not get past was that I did not know these people. Who was this man who said he was my husband? Just because he picked me up from the hospital doesn't mean that I belong to him. The kids were cute, but I didn't really feel a connection to them either.

Lucien turned to me at one point and said, "Marie is hungry, aren't you going to breast feed her?" I slowly bonded with my baby girl, by feeding her. And Megan was so adorable that with each passing day, we got closer and closer. She would also offer up useful hints by saying, "Mommy do you remember when you used to fold the clothes, and how you would put them in the draw this way?" Little by little my girls helped me piece my life together. My friends were also there supporting me. But the block with Lucien would remain.

While I was in the hospital, in between visits from Jimmy, Lucien had come for a visit. He said, "They are going to release you tomorrow, just in time for you to cook Easter dinner." I responded by asking who the hell he was. "That's not funny Trace, I'm your husband."

I replied sarcastically, "Was I a drug addict or alcoholic? What was wrong with me?" Lucien's reply, "Nothing. Now quit acting so stupid. I'll pick you up tomorrow." And he left.

In my own mind, I began to chalk up the whole experience with Jimmy as some kind of hallucination. I began to feel as if I were loosing my mind. It was easy, given the fact that the only encouragement I ever got from Lucien was to assure me that I was disturbed. I knew his family believed it to be true, and now, I was beginning to agree.

It had been a very long day, I was exhausted and looking forward to a good night's rest, but it was not to be. At eleven o'clock that evening, my friend Michelle called. Lucien hated the fact that we were friends. Not surprising since he often took a dislike to anyone who afforded me with positive encouragement. I never had anything in my life that was easy. My relationships with both family and friends alike would always be a struggle.

This fateful call was the beginning of my career as a psychic. Unknowingly, in helping my friend that night, I successfully gave my first reading.

Michelle called me up to chat and I commented that her home was unusually quiet. Michelle had three children, two boys and a girl. Her kids were a lot older than mine they were teenagers. I asked her, "Where is everybody?" She replied, "The boys are asleep, and Naomi is staying at a friend's house."

"No she isn't."

"Tracy, why would you say something like that?" Michelle asked.

I continued, "I don't know, she is not at a sleep-over, she's at the school. She's with a boy and wearing her new Victoria's Secret bra. She is planning on having sex for the first time!"

Michelle was getting a little upset and replied, "How could she, she's only sixteen years old! Why would you say something like this Tracy?"

"I don't know. It just came to me."

Michelle said she would call me back in a minute. Immediately after hanging up, she called her daughter's friend's mother. The one she was supposed to be sleeping over at. To her dismay the girl's mother confirmed the fact that she was not there, and that she never had any intention of coming over. The sleepover was never arranged.

Michelle realized as she hung up with the woman that her daughter had the whole night to be out and about without any worry that she would ever be discovered.

She called me back and informed me I was right and her daughter was not where she said she would be. Michelle decided to go out looking for her daughter. While driving through the neighborhood, she was talking with me on her cell phone trying to figure out to which school her daughter had gone. As I relayed more detail to her, I could hear Michelle muttering to herself, "I'm going to fucking kill her if she has already had sex!"

I interrupted and assured my friend, "No, you're okay. He's just getting to the bra now."

Completely unaware that I was even doing it, I was giving Michelle a play by play to the evening's events, right down to the smallest detail.

In the background I could hear Michelle get out of her car and begin running toward the unsuspecting couple, screaming, "Take your fucking hands off her, that's my baby!"

I could hear fighting and screaming, as well as Naomi asking, "How did you find me? How did you find me?"

Michelle began to explain to her startled daughter, "Since Tracy's near-death experience, she has all these psychic powers, and tonight she focused in on you." Michelle knew that I was psychic, but until that night had no idea how good I really was.

Still on the line holding patiently, I could hear Naomi asking, "Why me? Why me? Why did she pick me?" Unfortunately for Naomi, but fortunately for me, I needed to practice on someone.

From that moment on Michelle was going to watch her daughter like a hawk. This incident with me convinced Naomi to be on her best behavior.

In gratitude for what I did, Michelle mentioned to me that I needed to use my gift to help other people.

I became agitated at the thought, and told Michelle, "My husband would kill me. He would be so angry with me. I just don't have the strength to deal with him."

I explained to my friend that I was in debt upwards of sixty thousand dollars because of my many illnesses. We had paid the hospital, but Lucien felt I should pay him back that money as well. Lucien kept reminding me that I would have to pay him back every cent, but refused to allow me to hold down a real job and earn my own money. On the one hand he would say, "Go get a real job." and in the next moment he would say, "Why did you have kids, if you wanted a career?" he was always in control, and I was always wrong. To top it off, I was a young mother with two small children to raise and no one to care for them while I worked.

Michelle refused to give up and suggested, "You can work in my basement. You can do readings and keep the money. I'll help you get started."

I finally agreed. It wasn't long before word spread like wild fire. Business was booming, but at ten dollars a reading it would take a long time to pay Lucien back his money. Back then the only time I had available to do readings was while my girls napped.

Once I began doing readings, I was reunited with Jimmy who was my guide, but no longer the man in his seventies I remembered from the hospital. He was thirty-eight and even more handsome than I remembered. Jimmy was five ten with a slender build. He had strawberry blond hair, and the most captivating blue eyes one could ever imagine, with a smile to match.

So our new partnership began. I would look up at Jimmy, and he would give me all the answers to my clients' inquiries. The answers would come in the form of mini movies that I would visualize in my mind of my client's personal data. My clients would come in, and make themselves comfortable in a chair opposite me and would ask, "Tell me something about my life." I would oblige them, look up at Jimmy, and he would relate all that I needed to know, and I would repeat it to my client. This is how the guides got me started.

Time passed and I became more committed to my newfound trade. I wanted to learn more about other psychics, their mannerisms, and how they interacted with the public in general.

I decided to take a psychic development course. It was there that I made a new friend, Raphael. I walked into the class while he was in the midst of speaking with "Jesus", in front of a group of students. I was able to see the same image, and proceeded to finish his description of the entity before him, adding that he is wearing a red tunic with a purple belt, and a gold cloak around his shoulders.

Raphael turned to me and asked, "You see him? Really? You do? This is cool—we're not crazy." We high-fived each other, so happy that we both could see the same thing even though everyone else could not. The class was speechless.

After class, it was just Raphael and myself, both thrilled to have found someone who shared similar gifts.

Dear Reader, It is amazing to find someone who shares the same talent. For the first time I felt that I was not alone in the world.

As we sat down I mentioned to him, "Your guide is behind you. He is this beautiful man, wearing a white robe." He had reminded me of a Greek god, he was so beautiful.

Raphael said, "That's Al, he was my lover. He died six months ago."

As if to reciprocate the gesture, Raphael made me aware of my guide. "He is dressed in a military uniform from World War I, his name is Jimmy."

A little surprised I ask, "Jimmy is from World War I?"

Raphael continued, "Yes. You two were married in a past life, with two small girls. When he left you, he said he would come back to you but he couldn't. He was killed in a plane crash in that war, so he came back now."

On hearing these words I almost died of shock. "I had two kids when he left me, and I have two kids now." As I sat listening and absorbing all that my new friend was relating, I thought to myself, "Love does transcend all time." The new revelation that Jimmy was once my husband helped me reframe my experience at the hospital when we first met. More than ever I believed I had a purpose in life and I felt blessed.

It felt as if history were repeating itself. Here was Jimmy with me and our daughters once again. I was now more comfortable with my guide and enjoying my new life.

In comparison, with very little to compare to at that, my life with Lucien seemed more like a dream—and not a very good one. I had lost all memory of my prior life with Lucien, along with any feelings I may have once held for him.

Once I was home, Lucien took advantage of my memory loss. He told me, his estranged wife, that I would cook, clean, and serve him at his beck and call. I could only think that this was completely impossible, and couldn't help feeling as if I was living someone else's life, not my own. It would take me ten years of acupuncture and therapy for me to recall my memory, and then it was easy to understand why I had chosen to forget it. After all, ignorance is bliss.

I was living a new life with my spirit-guide husband, and it felt great. This went on for four years. People would come to see me for a reading and Jimmy would faithfully relate all that I needed to know. We were a great team. The day finally came when Jimmy explained to me that he would be leaving. At this point I was doing readings in my own home.

I couldn't believe what I was hearing, "You can't leave me!"

Jimmy told me that he could no longer stand to be away from me. He missed the physical connection. He needed to come back to the Earth plane and find me so that we could be together.

I became excited at the idea, "You could do that?"

Jimmy replied, "Yes, and all you'll need to know is Jimmy, 38, California, pilot."

And then he was gone. Just my luck, my soul mate is a spirit guide looking for a body. Personally, I hope he finds one, and soon.

When Jimmy first left, he was replaced with two new guides, an American Indian and an older woman, who was very wise. But they were not Jimmy, and it took me some time to get used to them. I still needed to work because I was building my business. I would work psychic fairs; aside from the money it was a wonderful way to get exposure.

On one particular day I was working a fair at a health food store. The store was upstairs, but the psychic fairs were held in the basement. I was enjoying a growing reputation, and the health food store had advertised my attendance at the fair. They were excited about the volume of people my name would draw to the event.

It was about four o'clock in the afternoon and I was waiting for my next client to arrive. All of a sudden I became very nauseous. I thought to myself, "I must have food poisoning." At the door, a guy magically appears as if out of thin air demanding, "Are you Tracy? I'm your four o'clock." I happened to glance up at the clock on the wall, and noticed its hands were moving in a counter-clockwise motion. Today I know that the mysterious stranger was a demon, but back then I just felt sick.

I stood up and said to this stranger, "I am so sorry, but I think I have food poisoning, can we reschedule for tomorrow?" The stranger was a towering six feet tall. He was dressed in camouflage and had cuts all over his body, as if he had just been in a fight. He looked at me and in a derogatory tone said, "A psychic turning down money? That's unheard of."

I said, "Please, I promise to come back tomorrow and read you, but right now, I just really feel sick and want to go home."

At that very moment, I noticed that the other psychics sharing the space with me had slowly huddled into a corner of the room, they were apparently afraid of this stranger. Instantly I felt this stranger inside of my head, reading my thoughts. I thought, "Oh my god, he must be psychic."

The man said to me, "I am going to take you home, rape you, and then slit your throat as you are running for the door."

In the hope of distracting his thoughts I replied, "You need to go to the top of some very tall mountains, collect your thoughts and write a book." After which, I ran home.

Dear Reader, Even though psychic abilities are a gift from God, this does not mean that the devils of this world won't try to get me to play for their team.

When I arrived home, my husband Lucien told me that a letter had arrived for me. When I opened up the letter, it read;

I am looking forward to you reading me tomorrow. I have heard that you are one of the best, and have travelled many miles to meet you. I hope you pass the test.

The letter was fashioned out of words cut from magazines. It looked like a ransom note. Highlighted in yellow were the words; *I am going to slit your throat.*

Lucien and I wasted no time in calling the police. The police advised me to go to the health food store as scheduled, and that they would be waiting in the parking lot to arrest him.

Later that evening, I was taking off my makeup in the upstairs bathroom when I heard my front door open. I heard a set of footsteps coming up the stairs, and I saw the stranger from the health food store. He appeared to be drunk because he was stumbling to keep his balance. I screamed and the stranger disappeared. It was at this moment that I realized he had to have been a ghost.

I ran to the phone and called my friend Raphael, my fellow psychic, and related the story to him. That very night, we went to the nearest church and loaded up on holy water, which we took with us to the fair the next day.

Raphael promised to stay by my side. With the aid of another psychic and the show *Charmed*, we utilized the power of three to vanquish the demon. The demonic spirit entered the building. The police were in the parking lot. The stranger came to the top of the basement stairs. I was holding hands with Raphael and the other psychic as the entity thundered, "Tracy, come to me." I yelled, "No," while clutching my friends' hands. The holy water that was on our table started to bubble. The stranger disappeared once and for all.

The police said that he entered the building, but never left. They did not understand what happened. He had arrived in an unmarked van with no license plate. Thank God for the holy water.

Chapter Seven

Signs of Jimmy Angel

*"How do I love thee? Let me count the ways. I love thee to
the depth and breadth and height My soul can reach..."*
—Elizabeth Barrett Browning,
Sonnets from the Portuguese

From the moment Michael related that Jimmy and I were married in a past life nothing would be the same again.

More than ever, I felt like my life had purpose.

Our story reads like a romance novel—two star-crossed lovers caught between time and space, each struggling to reconnect with the other.

True to his word, Jimmy remained with me for four years as my guide, helping to further my psychic career. But as my lost love, he was compelled to find a way back to me, which, ironically, meant leaving me again.

The four years flew by and Jimmy announced he was leaving. He reassured me others would be coming in his place to guide me, but it was time for him to come back to earth and find me. Before he left, he told me all I needed to know was, "Jimmy, 38, California, pilot." And with those words, Jimmy disappeared as quickly as he had appeared that Saturday morning at Mercy Hospital. I was left with a hole in my heart that, to this day, aches with longing for the man I had lost a lifetime ago.

The few years that Jimmy was a part of my life could not have been better. I was happy and life seemed to be running smoothly.

When Jimmy left I realized I was in a loveless marriage, and it was time to leave.

I was embarking upon an emotional roller coaster ride. How could I leave my husband for a spirit guide? Was I losing my mind? These thoughts plagued me to no end.

Staying with Lucien would have impeded my progress. I would not be the woman I am today if I did not find the courage to risk it all, and seek a better life for my daughters and myself.

Jimmy had assured me he would find me again. I thought at the time the clues that Jimmy had left behind were quite obvious. I believed that I would meet a guy from California named Jimmy and that he would be thirty-eight years old. Or it would be a flight number, and I would meet him on the plane en route to California. He would be thirty-eight and a pilot. Maybe the flight number was thirty-eight. What if I was flying to California to shoot a pilot for a television series based on my life, thirty-eight was a stage number, and I would meet him on the set. Maybe he moved thirty eight times.

My thoughts ran wild with possibilities, and for a time it gave me the motivation I needed to start life anew.

The others that Jimmy mentioned would come did. I was assigned new guides that came to help me, enabling me to continue with my work. I still owed my husband sixty thousand dollars in medical expenses, I still had a miserable life, and through it all, all I could think about was Jimmy. The dream was that he would come back and take me away to a better life, where I would be happy.

Summer was on its last legs and I was sitting around at home, figuring out what to make for dinner. I decided pesto sounded good. As I was getting the ingredients together, I realized that I did not have enough basil. My basil plants were starting to die. Always brilliant at improvising in a pinch, I added spinach instead. I took a package of spinach from the freezer, broke off a piece, ran it under some water, and threw it in the blender. Under normal circumstances, the desired result would be green in color. The pesto in my blender was clearly turning gray. In my mind I rationalized,

"I added green, this should be green." I decided to add more garlic and Parmesan cheese, but it just didn't taste right. I felt like I might have been fighting off a bug or getting sick again and that maybe what was affecting my taste buds. I continued to add more salt and garlic but nothing worked. I abandoned the pesto, and decided to just eat the spinach.

I fed the girls and Lucien spaghetti, while I continued eating the spinach. Throughout the meal between bites of spinach that did not taste right, I was distracted with thoughts of all the money I still owed my husband. I was wondering how I was going to get out of all that debt and thinking I would really have to do a lot more readings. With a crunch, my mind was suddenly back on my meal. "What the hell am I eating? Does my spinach have nuts?" In my head, my guides are all abuzz, "You're going to be rich, you're going to be rich, a lot of money coming, you're going to be rich!"

But I was only getting more and more irritated. My thoughts were swinging back and forth like a pendulum, between thinking my guides may have been lying to me, to whatever was now cutting into my gums.

I pulled what looked to be a branch out of my mouth. I turned to my husband and asked, "Lucien, is this a branch? Is there a branch in my spinach? "You know I don't see well."

He started to laugh and laugh some more. "Why are you laughing so hard?"

"It's not a branch you blind bitch," he continued, his words seething with hatred toward me. "It's the fucking paw of a rat!"

It was, in fact, the whole leg that was scraping at my gums. Lucien's laughter continued as he told me, "You ate a rat, and we're going to be rich."

He promptly went into the kitchen and started picking through the spinach, calling out to me his various discoveries, "Snout, paw...", collecting his new found treasure into a plastic bag. Never once stopping to inquire about how I was doing. I quietly went to the bathroom and started throwing up.

Returning from the bathroom, Lucien still happily collecting his exhibits, I called the CDC (Centers for Disease Control). I related to them my fear; I was a nursing mother, with no spleen, who had just eaten a rat. The representative started laughing, thinking the call was just a prank. They realized quickly that it was not. Concerned, they asked me my age, when I had my spleen removed, and general background questions. And yet, after all was said and done, they were at a loss as to how to advise me. I was the first of such incidents reported to the CDC. Without knowing any better, they told me I would probably develop some form of cancer, and that I should call them back to let them know what happens. I did become quite ill, my menstrual cycles became irregular, and I experienced nausea and fatigue for months to come.

After surviving the night, Lucien and I solicited the help of a lawyer. It was a difficult ordeal for me to endure. My lawsuit made all the local papers. I began to receive death threats. I developed an eating disorder because I was afraid to eat anything. I only ate whole foods, a piece of bread, apples, things that I could see would not offer up any surprises. All of this proved to be too much. I did not want to go through with the lawsuit, I wanted to settle. This new nightmare had to end.

My lawyer hired a forensic team to study the DNA of the rat I had eaten. As a side note, they were the very same people used in O.J. Simpson's murder trial. The team revealed it was not a rat, but a family of shrews. On the opposing side, they hired a psychologist in their defense to prove that I was the one that had a problem.

News flash—I would think anyone eating spinach and finding a family of shrews instead would have a problem.

While I was enduring the interrogation, the defendant's therapist had the audacity to express, "You eat protein don't you, chicken, cow and such?"

I replied, "I take the feathers off the chicken, the snout and the eyeballs off the cow, and I cook that nondescript piece of protein until I barely know what I am eating. I don't drink the blood or chew the bones. Need I remind you, the rat was raw? I was making pesto!"

The therapist answered, as he clicked his recorder to record, "Note to self, the client has no problem eating protein."

I took a deep breath, and tried very hard to contain the anger welling up inside me but I psychically blew a fuse. I proceeded to tell the therapist that his dead grandmother was present and that she had a message for her grandson. She did not pay for his college to have him stoop so low and distort the law to make a buck. She felt that her grandson was better than that, and reminded him that she was watching. He was clearly spooked.

The therapist called my attorney and said, "We are willing to settle this case." He then placed his hand over the receiver, looked over at me and said, "What did I ever do to you?" He was scared to death and white as a ghost. I am sure, prior to this meeting, the therapist thought he had a sure win on his hands. I recalled, while filling out all of his paperwork, one of the questions asked was, "Do you hear voices?" To which I obviously replied, "Yes."

I was eventually awarded one hundred thousand dollars. After the lawyers took their share, and the outstanding bills were paid, I was left with sixty thousand dollars. I gave the check to Lucien and said, "Debt paid." At this point in my marriage, I was ready to leave.

Though my guides have never left me, they have never told me what I should do in regard to my own life decisions. They have always encouraged me to rely on my own faith and this is their greatest test of my character. As a young mother of two, the prospect of supporting myself and my two daughters on my psychic talent was weighing down hard on my thoughts as I struggled to plan my next move.

I thought, before ending my marriage, I would take the whole family, including my parents, to Disney World, since they had never been. It was the month of January. While staying in one of the resort hotels, on a particularly cold morning, I met my father down in the lobby. I looked at him and said, "You look tired and sick."

His birthday was just around the corner and I asked him, "Dad, how old are you going to be? 58?"

He replied, "I am only going to be 56, why do you ask?"

I turned to him nonchalantly and said, "At the age of 58 you are going to die, and I didn't want it to be my fault because of this cold weather." (My father had a heart condition).

My father responded by asking me, "Why would you say something so mean?"

"I'm sorry, I shouldn't have said anything." Too late, the damage was done.

It was my wish for my guides to grant me enhanced abilities. I interpreted their constant testing as their way of asking me, "Can you handle it?" By passing their many tests with my faith intact I felt that I could handle any gift they chose to endow me with. To be the warrior I often claimed myself to be, I would always need to accept these tests without question. Although my guides may seem tough, they are not without a sense of humor, especially when they choose to give me a clue about what my next step should be.

The one thing my guides related to me before we moved from New York down to Florida, where my parents lived, was that Lucien was not to be a part of my future. I needed to leave him. This was supposed to be a fresh start for both of us. It was very obvious to me. He had his money and everything was in his name. I would have to start over and I was going to focus on my readings.

Looking back, I recalled the reading that jump-started my new life. Lucien never cared for my talent, but if it brought in money, he would grudgingly accept it.

A woman came over to our house for a reading. She mentioned to me that she was hard of hearing and that we would have to talk very loud. Great! Lucien was in the next room, already hating it, and now he would have to hear it in stereo. And so it went, I would reveal a piece of psychic information, to which the woman would reply, very loudly, "What did you say?" I would proceed to tell her again, and the woman would whisper her own little psychic gems such as, "Listen to me, get a bank account; save your money; by

June you must be gone." After which she would say, "What did you say?"

My guide was talking through an older woman, and all the while I had no clue this was happening. At first I was a bit bewildered, wondering who was reading whom. I proceeded to read her again, and again the woman whispered, "If you don't leave him now, you will never fulfill your destiny. You'll never become what you are supposed to be." And then in a very loud voice, she asked, "So how are my husband and I going to do in Vegas?"

I often laugh when recollecting this reading. I was as confused as my client. I didn't know whether the woman was messing with me. But the woman would always insist, "I don't know what you are talking about—remember I said I was hard of hearing, so you need to speak very loud so I can hear you."

I didn't know whether the woman was suffering with a multiple personality disorder, or if she was just crazy. In any event, I chose to play along. As I continued reading my client, it became apparent to me that this experience literally felt like the angels were pushing me out the door, giving me no other option except to leave and never look back.

That day, I made the decision to leave Lucien. It would be one of the hardest things I would ever do. And it has been hard for me ever since. Lucien has never passed on an opportunity to let me forget it either. There were times when I questioned my own actions, calling my own sanity to task. "What have I done?" I would ask myself. "I've uprooted my children, I have no financial resources of my own, I have to start from scratch, I gave him the house, and now I'm moving in with my mother."

As I sat in the car crying, listening to Casey Kasem playing on the radio in the background, I continued to question my decision. "What am I doing?" I asked myself. "I've destroyed so many lives, for what? For passion, a dream, a fantasy? I'm in love with a ghost!"

That's when the dedication came through on the radio. My attention was brought back to Casey Kasem announcing, "A long distance dedication from Jimmy to Tracy, *Feels Like the First Time,* by Foreigner." As the music began to fill the car, the lyrics washed over me, a welcome salve, bringing me peace and assurance:

> *"I would climb any mountain*
> *Sail across a stormy sea*
> *If that's what it takes me baby*
> *To show how much you mean to me And I guess it's just the woman in*
> *you That brings out the man in me*
> *I know I can't help myself*
> *You're all the world to me*
>
> *It feels like the first time*
> *It feels like the very first time...*
> *I would have waited a lifetime*
> *Spent my time so foolishly*
> *But now I've found you*
> *Together we'll make history..."*

My heart leapt. I thought, "It has got to be from him, he's talking to me. The show is based out in California, this is a sign— it's Jimmy."

And so it would go, whenever I started to lose faith I would always receive a sign, heaven-sent, from my beloved Jimmy.

As I began my struggle to become financially independent, juggling career and motherhood, my faith would be tested. But there would always be another sign.

Three years had passed since leaving Lucien and life was still challenging. I became a Girl Scout Brownie leader for my daughter, Megan's, troop. This particular meeting found me very distracted, my mind burdened with my financial worries, when Maggie the troop leader said, "Tracy, your group is doing Venezuela, and your focus will be Angel Falls. Do you know the story?"

I did not. In the course of helping Megan with her research, I quickly became familiar with another Jimmie Angel.

This Jimmie Angel was also a talented aviator, born in the United States. He served in World War I and then went to work as an independent contract pilot. He had a taste for adventure and a particular attraction to Venezuela, where he spent much of his time.

As I learned while helping my daughter in her research, Jimmie Angel is credited with the discovery of what would later be known to the world as Angel Falls, the highest waterfall in the world. Interestingly enough, Angel Falls is located in an area, translated from the language of the indigenous Pemon people, to mean "House of the Devil." My battle between good and evil has always been fought upon a very thin line. Was this a clue or a distraction?

Jimmie Angel's airplane rested atop Auyán-tepui, the location of Angel Falls, for thirty-three years after his plane became stuck in the soft earth on a return visit. The Venezuelan government declared it a national monument in 1964.

*Dear Reader, The plane was resting atop that mountain for thirty-three years, not thirty-eight. One thing that I have learned from my work with my angels is that they are extremely accurate, with no margin for error. The only errors made, are **human**.*

Jimmie Angel died December 8, 1956 from complications after an airplane crash. His cremated remains are entombed in the Portal of the "Folded Wings", an aviation memorial in Burbank, California.

Jimmie had many things in common with what I know about my true love, but he was not the one. However, in my mind it was yet another sign from my Jimmy, asking me to hang in there and to have faith that we would be reunited.

But at the end of the day we are all just human, and in our humanness we forge forward in this life with a certain vulnerability. We want so much to find love and be happy, that our judgment sometimes becomes compromised.

It was during one of those lapses in judgment that I met Constantine. He was thirty-eight. We were attracted to each other and so I tried to make him be Jimmy. I convinced myself that he fit the profile. Ignoring my guides, I walked myself straight into a hell that made Lucien look like Prince Charming, but that's another chapter.

The last clue I was given was in the form of a young boy, James Leininger of Baton Rouge, Louisiana. His parents were on *Good Morning America* promoting their book *Soul Survivor: The Reincarnation of a World War II Fighter Pilot.*

It was written in defense of their belief that their son, in a past life, was a World War II pilot. Right around the time that their child had turned two years of age, he began to have vivid nightmares of dying in a plane crash over water. He also had an uncanny familiarity with fighter planes from that era that he documented with drawings. After seeking help for their child, the Leiningers' were able to deduce after two very long years that their son was in fact reliving the death of a Lt. James McCready Huston. Huston was a twenty one year old Navy pilot who died during World War II, when his plane was shot down over the Pacific in 1945.

Today, as I look back, I often wonder whether I will ever meet Jimmy again. My faith assures me that I will, but my mind continues to entertain doubts and test my patience. The thought is like a scar that smarts at the very thought of never seeing Jimmy again. It is at these times that I comfort myself with the knowledge that my angels only speak the truth and I continue to learn to think outside the box. I hope to have this mystery solved by the end of this book. Maybe my Jimmy will meet me at a book signing.

Every time I start to get depressed, I am given the gift of hope. Maybe it is a reward for the commitment I have made to my guides and my talent. They will always offer me a reciprocal gesture by bringing to my attention something that will reaffirm the fact that all heaven and earth are orchestrating the reunion with my one true love. Jimmy and myself.

One can certainly marvel at the inner workings of the human mind and our capacity to love. It truly seems to transcend both time and space. For me this is common knowledge by virtue of just being psychic and using my talents to help countless people. I was beginning to feel like Goldilocks, the first Jimmy was too old, and the second, too young, I hope my Jimmy will be just right.

It is our collective hope to believe in something greater than ourselves, and that we are meant for bigger things. Yet we don't always heed the signs and we lose our way. But if we take the time to pay attention, if we are patient and keep the faith, as Eleanor Roosevelt so elegantly put it, "It is better to light the candle than to curse the darkness."

And as I write these words, I know in my own heart that I will one day find Jimmy because just when you think he is gone, suddenly, there he is.

Chapter Eight

Your Friendly
Neighborhood Psychic

"We do not need magic to transform our world. We carry
all of the power we need inside ourselves already."
—J.K. Rowling

No matter where I live, my neighbors quickly learn that I am different. After a while, my psychic ability just seems to ooze through the neighborhood, affecting various lives, even though they may never come for an actual reading.

Back when I was living in New York and still married to Lucien it was common for different religious groups to go door-to-door hoping to find new recruits. On this particular day, the Mormons were the religious group of choice.

At my door were Elder Walker and Elder Chen. I welcomed them into my home, mostly because I was in need of some adult chitchat. My children were still very young. In the midst of our conversation, they learned about my psychic abilities. So they began asking me, "What makes you think that you are psychic?" Elder Walker wanted me to guess his first name. As I focused on him to get his name, my mind started to wander and I was recalling a TV show that I watched when I was kid. I began to target on the character Duane. As it turns out, this was Elder Walker's first name.

By now Elder Chen, just as curious, turned to me and said, "Surprise me." I responded by holding up my hand with five fingers extended, and then I added another two fingers denoting a separation. I said to him that this means five children and then another two children, but I don't understand the separation. To which Elder Chen replied, "My mother had five children of her own and adopted two."

Elder Chen was floored by my insight. At this point they both decided they wanted to make me a Prophet to represent their church. After their meeting with me, they were convinced I was the real deal.

Before becoming a Prophet, there were a few requirements I had to meet. I had to give up caffeine, alcohol, and cursing. This may sound simple enough to some people, but for me they may as well have asked that I move to Siberia. This was by no means a subtle change for me. I did pretty well with the vulgarity and the alcohol, but I really had trouble with the caffeine. I eventually gave up that too, which lead to my baptism into their church.

This new lifestyle lasted only a week. The coffee was first to make its way back, followed by alcohol, and finally the cursing. I gave my last speech to the church, mostly to let them know they would need to find someone else to fill my spot. I personally couldn't understand why God would have a problem with caffeine. I ended with a few choice words, and headed off to get a much needed drink. Wasn't it enough that I was psychic?

Following Elder Walker and Elder Chen's visit and my subsequent baptism into their church my neighbor made a comment and asked, "How do you like your new position at the church?" I laughed and related to her the previous evening's events. My neighbor Mandy was a "wild child" in her own right. She wouldn't have lasted a minute, let alone a week.

While I was standing there looking at her, I had a premonition her husband was going to attempt to kill her. I told her that on the day that she would be murdered, she would be wearing a short shirt that would reveal her abdomen, and a pair of tight jeans. She looked at me in utter disbelief and said, "I don't even own an outfit like that, and my Mike would never hurt me."

Fast forward a few months later, Mandy had found a new job as a waitress at a local bar. She ended up having a fling with the owner and then caught a little something, which she brought home to Mike.

As she was relating to me how mad her husband was at her, I told her, "Mandy, you are wearing the short shirt, with the tight jeans, I thought you said you didn't own an outfit like this." She gasped and explained that another friend had cleaned out her closet and given her these clothes. She began to cry and said, "Mike did say he was going to kill me, oh my God, what should I do?" I decided to put Mandy up for a couple of weeks, giving her husband time to cool down. After that, they sought counseling to try and salvage their marriage. Nobody dies on my watch!

Dear Reader, Some premonitions can be changed. Not all are written in stone.

Back home in New York, life was slowly returning to normal after being sick. I was walking Megan to school one morning, pushing Marie in the stroller, when I saw another mother with long, dark hair. She had one child Megan's age and triplets that were Marie's age. Still learning the many nuances of tact, I walked over to this woman and asked abruptly, "Why won't you do anything about your breast cancer especially since your own mother died when you were only four years old?" I continued yelling at her, "Don't do this to your children!"

She hauled off and slapped me across the face. "Crazy lady, you are scaring my children!"

A couple of weeks had passed and I happened to see this young mother again. This time, she was making her way toward me. I felt a little apprehensive, not in the mood to get my face slapped again. I relaxed as I noticed the smile on her face. She came to thank me. She recognized an element of truth from our first encounter and acted on my advice. She went and got herself a mammogram. They found the cancer and removed it. She had mentioned she was afraid to go, but was happy I made her. Despite my obvious lack of tact initially, we became great friends.

We started hanging out together, walking our babies everywhere. On this particular occasion, we decided to stop at a local restaurant to have a drink and hang out. We noticed the establishment had one of those slot machines for the entertainment of their customers. We each invested a dollar, the most our respective budgets would allow. I used my psychic ability and, *abracadabra*, out came a hundred. We decided very quickly that this was not the way to spend our afternoon. We divided our winnings and took our babies home.

Dear Reader, My grandmother told me when I first became aware of my psychic ability that I could not use it for self-gain or gambling. She told me that if I continued to misuse it I would lose it. It is only for the greater good of mankind.

It wasn't any different when I moved to Florida. Again word of my psychic abilities seemed to slowly spread and my skills began affecting the lives of those around me. I was new in the neighborhood, and, at this time, still married to Lucien. It would be another year before we were separated and I could have a new beginning.

Trying to make new friends, I went jogging alongside one of my neighbors, my mouth running as fast as my feet. Tara, my neighbor, began to tell me a story about how her husband's boss was murdered. They had no leads or suspects. I volunteered to do a séance for the dead man, in hopes of finding his killer. I thought this would make me fast friends with my new neighbor. I should mention I had never done a séance before. However, I had seen them do it on the T.V. show *Charmed*, so I thought I would just take a cue from them.

I went to the dead man's home and met with a few of his ex-wives. He was apparently very wealthy and quite the ladies man. I sat everyone in a circle and asked them to hold hands. I said a little prayer and invited the dead man into my body. What happened next shocked the hell out of me.

It was like a switch was flipped, instantaneously sending electricity coursing through my veins and conducting its way to everyone in the circle. And then I became the deceased, seeing with his eyes, learning what had become of him.

A lady friend gave him a drink and then he started to feel woozy. I had heard some of the ex-wives comment that he was a recovering alcoholic, but it turned out that this drink had drugs in it, not alcohol. As he was making his way to his home, he saw the lady friend he had just left with one of her friends. He turned to her, and asked, "How did you beat me here?" She replied, "I must drive faster." Now inside, becoming weaker by the minute, he proceeded to sit down in an orange, crushed velvet, chair. The next thing he noticed were his curtains on fire in front of him. He tried to move, but couldn't. The drug cocktail had paralyzed him. He wasn't even able to take his last breath.

I closed the séance to a bevy of emotion. Some people were amazed while others were in disbelief. I went home thinking it was a job well done. No sooner did I arrive home, there was a knock at my door. There were two detectives that wanted to bring me downtown. They put me in handcuffs and lead me out to their patrol car. In the background I could hear Lucien say, "This is why I don't like this shit!"

Downtown at the station, they did the usual, "Where were you the night of… " routine. Lucky for me I was back in New York, packing my house up to move down to Florida. They asked me how I knew that he did not take his last breath. To which I replied, "That's easy, I was doing a séance and the deceased man inhabited my body."

They said, "Only two people knew that he had no smoke in his lungs, you and the man who performed the autopsy."

They were very nice and let me go. They turned to me and added, "Come back if you can figure out who murdered him."

Now an expert in séances, I volunteered to remove the ghost of a little girl from a local restaurant. I had become friends with a local newspaper reporter and she thought this would make a good piece. It had been fifty years since that child was killed in front of the restaurant by a car. She was only five years old. Her red ball had rolled out into the street and she was quick to pursue it. This séance was more professional, unlike my last one.

The séance circle was made up of Samantha, the local news reporter, the deceased girl's father, a few of the old employees that had worked in the restaurant at the time of her death, and myself. We had a cassette recorder in the middle of the circle and a video recorder set-up outside the circle. Once again, my body was host to the deceased spirit. The little girl began to speak through me, but more than that, I actually sounded like her and assumed the mannerisms of this five-year-old child. I was able to successfully convince this child that she was, in fact, dead and helped her cross over.

Once the séance was complete the unexplainable started to manifest itself to all those present. We played back the cassette recording. What it captured was more than any of us could have imagined. It recorded the actual accident, playing back in real-time. We heard the little girl's screams, the car screeching to a halt before hitting her, and the ensuing screams from the crowd in the background. We then decided to play back the video, not knowing what to expect. We were even more surprised at what we saw. There were two spirits encircling our group, floating eerily around us. I believe that those two spirits thought they would be invited next to join the séance. They had nothing to do with the little girl.

Still trying to meet new acquaintances, I inadvertently became friends with one of my clients, Jane, a veterinarian. During her reading, her deceased father came through. At the end she was left feeling sad and missing him. Seeing her so sad, I offered to do a séance to give her a chance to connect with her father.

While channeling her father, I began to feel my vocal chords on my throat being pulled at. Only they weren't mine, it felt instead that there was another set. I then heard a man's deep voice coming out of my body. Jane had also hooked me up to a machine that would monitor my pulse. While he continued talking through me, the monitor flat-lined. My pulse was gone! Jane was squeezing my hand and I squeezed back. Once the spirit left my body, I realized that I had learned something from this experience. There couldn't be two pulses existing in the same body, so while the spirit was in my body his pulse was detected, and as soon as the spirit left it read mine. This would be one of the last séances that I would ever do. The experience was unsettling for me. I felt like I was loosing control of my own body.

On my own, I did further research on what happened to me that night, particularly with the two sets of vocal chords. I found that we all have a second set that we don't use unless we are being possessed, or allowing a spirit to inhabit our bodies. Tibetan monks use the second set of vocal chords, or laryngeal folds, to create a harmonic sound, which I believe to be the universal language.

Chapter Nine

Daddy's Little Girl

"Certain is it that there is no kind of affection so purely angelic as of a father to a daughter. In love to our wives there is desire; to our sons, ambition; but to our daughter there is something which there are no words to express."
—Joseph Addison

I nherited my abilities from my father's mother, Celia. But, this wasn't a good thing. My father was never proud of his mother's ability, he would refer to the "old lady" as being nuts. The last thing he ever wanted was a crazy little girl.

Over the years, there were many instances where I would predict the future and it would come true. Usually the result of this was that I ended up grounded for using my abilities (or one could say for being honest)! At that point in my life I had no control over it. Maybe my father was a bit frightened by what I could do.

One Halloween night my dad was hanging out at the neighborhood bar. I walked in, dressed for the occasion as a very scary looking witch. No one looked twice as I walked up to my father and gave him a kiss on the cheek. I said in a giddy voice, "Hi daddy." My father turned to everyone and said, "This is my little girl." Again, no one paid much attention to us. I looked up at the various television sets broadcasting different sporting events. I proceeded to call out all the winners of every event, including scores, from horse races to football games. Then I walked out. Each one was predicted accurately, gaining the attention of the previously uninterested old men. They were paying attention now and wanted the witch back.

The next time I entered that bar I had blond hair and looked every bit the part of a "Suzy homemaker." Nobody believed it was

Tracy dressed as a witch for Halloween

the same girl, until I began to call out the results of the sporting events playing on the various screens.

Helping old men win sporting events was not my calling, but it did help endear myself to my dad. During those moments I carved out a little place for myself in his heart. That day, my dad was proud of his psychic daughter for the first time. I saw the joy in his eyes.

I would go on to predict, among other things, the year my brother would marry and the year my parents would move from New York to Florida. I also predicted the death of my father. Recalling that fateful family trip to Disney World, during my father's 56th birthday, I am astonished at how accurately my predictions unfolded.

Not long after that vacation, (more specifically, two years to the very date of that prediction) I moved down to Florida permanently. Just in time to help with my dad.

Walking along the beach with my father one day, he told me he had been urinating blood. I proceeded to read my father, completing a scan of his body, and told him that his bladder was filled with black, mucky stuff. Following my advice, he went to see a urologist.

After the exam, the urologist said, "Your bladder is filled with black, mucky stuff." To which my father responded by saying, "My psychic daughter used those exact same words, you would think a doctor would have used different ones."

The diagnosis was cancer of the bladder. They removed his bladder and prostate, and fitted him with a colostomy bag. This depressed my father to no end. He could no longer experience some of life's simple pleasures. His life had dramatically changed forever.

Not long after his last surgery, my father returned to the hospital to have knee surgery. It went well enough but his recovery was filled with unimaginable pain. The medication he was given had little affect. The doctor's response was that my father simply had a low threshold for pain.

On our way to a routine follow-up visit, I was helping my father out of the car when there was a sudden snap. My father fell to the ground in excruciating pain from his knee. At five feet and 2 inches, I carried my father's six-foot frame into the hospital to see the doctor. Love can truly move mountains!

When the doctor came in to see us, he looked at my father and had the same response. "He's just being a baby and can't handle pain." However the opposite was true. My father had the ability to handle great amounts of physical and emotional pain. Something we both have in common.

On the way home from the hospital, my father turned to me and said, "Hey little girl, would you buy me a bottle of cognac?" and added, "Maybe I am just a pussy." In reality he had snapped his kneecap. Something the doctor had failed to notice.

When we finally arrived home, my father proceeded to drink his pain away. Like father, like daughter. I began to read my father again and said, "I think the cancer has spread to your bones, you have bone cancer."

"Do you have a death wish for me?" he asked.

I replied, "You know dad, if I could save you from cancer, you would be hit by a car."

It seems as if when we fix one thing, something else will happen. Death was knocking on the door, and loudly. My father finished his bottle of cognac but the pain was relentless and unbearable. Nothing compares to the pain of having to watch a loved one suffer and being completely helpless in affording them solace.

I returned to the hospital with my father, but this time I became "Ms. Jekyll." I screamed at the doctors in attendance that I believed his cancer had come back, he may have bone cancer, and because of this he had damaged his kneecap. The doctors, taking things more seriously this time, ran a slew of tests. A few hours later, they returned to announce that my father had stage four bone cancer and only four weeks to live.

The doctors were very sorry. They confirmed that my father had broken his knee into seven pieces. Fragile from the cancer raging war on his body, it shattered. No amount of cognac could relieve the pain that he had endured.

I took my father home to die and that was where our miracle started. My father and I spent his last moments together playing "identify the dead person." I always had the ability to see spirits, it was no novelty for me but on his deathbed my father also acquired the ability. The game began when two spirits entered the room and my father turned to me asking who they were.

"Dad, that's Grandma and Grandpa," I told him. "Don't you recognize your Mom and Dad?"

"Of course I do. I was just testing to see how good you really are."

And so it would go, father and daughter would pass the hours taking turns identifying the spirits. Mostly they were deceased family members or, on a few occasions a celebrity, and we let them stay. Sometimes we would have unwelcome visitors and my father would say to them, "Be gone with you." He wasn't able to see them as well as I could but I would help him out. The game went on for days.

I felt, rather than saw, a strange presence enter the room and asked my father, "Who is this?"

My father said, "This is John."

"Then why can't I see him?"

"He is strictly here for me, he is my guide." I may not have been able to see him, but I would be able to hear him. He would also end up helping me.

Not quite a year after my father's passing, on a cold, November night, I came down with a fever that was rising rapidly. My mother, who was more often than not my nurse, found my fever to be uncontrollable, and went to the supermarket for some medicine. My eyes were bulging out of my head, I couldn't even touch my chin to my chest. My mother guessed that I probably had contracted meningitis from a mosquito during a visit to New York.

While my mother was at the store, my fever was ravaging my body and causing me to shake uncontrollably as I lay on my couch. Prior to leaving, my mother had placed an ice pack on my head and said, "I'll be back in fifteen minutes." That felt like an eternity. The ice didn't last five minutes and warm water soon began to run down my face.

As the fever wore on I felt as if I was losing consciousness. Between shivering and burning up, and feeling pain throughout every inch of my body, I thought to myself, "I can't take it anymore, I'm giving up." Then I heard a loud, male voice resounding through the room saying, "This is John, your father's guide. Although you can't see me, I am here to save your life. Reach down deep inside yourself and fight. We'll do this together."

Dear Reader, Our *will* is one of the greatest resources that we have at our *disposal.*

I did as I was told. My mother returned with medicine and miraculously I made it through to the next day. John had a message for my mother as well. He told her he wouldn't let her lose both her husband and her child so close to one another. If I know my father, I'm sure he put his guide up to this.

One of the blessings that came from the last few weeks I spent with my father was a greater understanding between us. My father apologized for not believing in my gift sooner and told me I was very good at what I did.

I would have done anything to save my father. I tried everything I knew within my power. I prayed over him and tried to heal him but to no avail. Nothing worked.

Finally, out of desperation, I invoked who I believed to be the entity Jesus Christ into my own body, in an attempt to save my father. The spirit did not enter my body but, instead, appeared at my father's bedside. I was lifted into the air by two celestial beings, and began floating just above my father's body.

He looked up at me and said, "You're hovering over me, you're going to fall and hurt me."

"Can't you see the angels holding me up Daddy?"

Jesus said to my father, "Bill, your time on earth is done. It's time for you to come home." My father agreed.

Jesus then turned to me, and said, "There are some things that you cannot fix, and this is one of them."

The angels put me back on the floor and they disappeared with Jesus. My father asked me, "Can you please cross me over to the other side?"

I told him I couldn't. I didn't think that was something I would be able to do. "You can do anything," He said and added, "I believe in you."

Instinctively I placed my left hand over his heart and felt his pulsing heart jump into the palm of my hand. I took his left hand with my right to aid him in the dying process. My father quietly slipped into a coma.

I called my mother and aunt into the room, and continued to hold his hand. Speaking on his behalf, I proceeded to relay a message to both my mother and aunt. Messages only they would understand

and know. I related to my mother the first thing my father had told her on their first date. He had a similar message for her sister. It was his way of saying goodbye.

I turned to my mother and said to her she would have to physically separate my father and me after I helped him cross over because I didn't think I could.

My father and I went through what felt like an underground tunnel that lead to a manhole. We pushed the manhole cover aside and looked out over what I believed to be the entrance to heaven. It was incredibly peaceful, reminiscent of my experience in the cave. There was an unusual stillness to this place but it was not an earthly sensation. If we could remember what it felt like to be in the womb, I imagine this is how it would feel. It was very natural, I felt no fear or sadness about my father dying.

My father climbed out, putting a hand on my shoulder and gently pushing me back down. I wasn't allowed to follow him. I stayed back, my head peeking out of the hole, and saw my father walk over to two beautiful gates. His parents were standing there, awaiting his arrival. He turned, placed his hand to his lips blowing me one last kiss, and waved goodbye.

Putting his arms around his parents, he walked through the Gates of Heaven. I had given my father the most precious of gifts, he did not have to die alone.

The next thing I knew my poor mother was slapping my face and attempting to pull my father's hand away from my grip. She was shouting at me, "Wake up, wake up!" She was holding my ice-cold hands, as a hospice nurse was declaring my father dead.

The nurse proceeded to take my pulse and said, "You're almost dead, we need to get you to the emergency room."

"No," I replied. "I'm just coming back."

I related the whole experience to the nurse, who stayed by my side, waiting for my pulse to get stronger. She confided to me that it was the most peaceful death she had ever witnessed. She would eventually become a client.

Two weeks later, I was back to my normal self and armed with a new found strength based on the belief that my father truly believed in my gift. His spirit has been with me every day since.

Tracy with her father on her wedding day

His gift was one of substantiation for the little girl who had spent her entire life trying to please her daddy.

Just when I think he has crossed over and moved on, he visits me in the form of a spirit. He is elated that I can see him.

Dear Reader, Here's the deal with spirits, they don't sleep and they don't eat, which means they are with you twenty four-seven, fresh as daisies.

At first, my father was having alcohol and cigarette withdrawals. And I, the ever helpful and very accommodating child, allowed his spirit to inhabit my body so that he could indulge his vices. I guess heaven is an alcohol and smoke free zone. On the other hand, I never smoked a day in my life. After two weeks of smoking like a chimney and drinking whiskey like a fish I had enough. I finally said, "Daddy, please, you are ruining my body, you have to leave." And so he did. Even though he left my body he was not ready to leave the house. He had some unfinished business and needed my help to play the part of the hopeless romantic to his widow.

He had promised my mother a Krugerrand coin. The Krugerrand coin was first minted in South Africa in 1967. It was the first gold coin to weigh precisely one ounce of gold. It had been my father's dying wish to present her with this rare keepsake along with thirty-five red roses, one for each year of their marriage. My mother loves long-stem, red roses. Many years later, thieves would relieve my mother of her precious coin.

Dear Reader, *The dead are not to be feared. It is the living that present us with challenges.*

So I once again I agree to help out my dad and obtain these gifts, only I didn't have any money. I turned to my father's spirit and said, "I need to work and make some money." All of a sudden, business picked up and I was able to fulfill my father's dying wish to my mother. Years later we still receive little miracles letting us know that Dad is around and thinking of us.

Four years later, my veterinarian friend/client and I were at a holiday party. We had been drinking and feeling good, when we were approached by a couple of guys that had invited us to their place for an "after party." I excused myself to use the facilities and said, "I'll be right back." While in the bathroom, sitting on the throne, my father appears. He was sitting on the edge of the bathtub and said, "Those guys are going to take you and your friend home, drug you, and rape you. Come on, I didn't raise you to be this way. Grab your friend and go home."

I emerged from the bathroom fifteen minutes later, white as a ghost, and said to my friend, "My dad says that we need to leave."

My friend turns to the two guys and says, "Her dad is dead, and when he says to leave, we listen. We gotta go."

My dad's spirit still visits, but not as often now. He only comes around when needed.

Chapter Ten

A Case of Mistaken Entity

"If your heart acquires strength, you will be able to remove blemishes from others without thinking evil of them."
—Mahatma Gandhi

I met him at the local bar. He was a tall and handsome stranger. A Greek god to be exact. He stood at six feet, with a muscular build, dark hair, a chiseled jaw, green eyes, and a movie star smile which he knew how to use. When our eyes met, I felt our attraction to one another. It wasn't long before we were talking and getting to know the other person a little better. I learned that he was recently out of rehab.

While we were having drinks, I thought to myself, Wow! What will power. Just out of rehab, and he can stop at two Bloody Mary's!

What I didn't know at the time was that he was in a drug rehabilitation program for crack-cocaine. Even so, drinking alcohol isn't on any "twelve-step road to recovery program" that I am aware of.

The night was pure magic as this charming thirty-eight year old from Chicago proceeded to sweep me off of my feet. It was a Harlequin romance in the making. Thoughts of Jimmy, 38, California, and pilot swam in my head. I rationalized that Chicago and California both start with the letter "C" so this could be him. He was the right age.

My angels tried to warn me that this was not the man for me but it was easy to convince myself that, in this case, they (my angels)

92

must be mistaken. Except angels never are. It was easy to ignore all the signs because in my heart I wanted to believe, I needed to believe, that this was my Jimmy. I wanted it so badly that I was blind to all the red flags going up around me like fireworks on the fourth of July. Everyone loves a bad boy!

With each turn on the dance floor, gazing into each other's eyes, the chemistry between us was undeniable. Everything seemed to click; his words were music to my ears. I never stood a chance. I had already fallen; hook, line, and sinker!

He painted an attractive picture that he was a brilliant and successful businessman, driving a BMW, living a wonderful life, with all these incredible things. But the nature of his business was never quite clear and he did not have a driver's license. He was brilliant all right. A brilliant con artist. His charm won me over and I fell hard. He made me many promises about our future life together and I was ready. I wanted love and I was going to make it happen.

Constantine and I were together for a total of three years. The relationship evolved from him trying to con me, to me trying to save him from himself. I thought I could change him. I almost did. In the end, as ironic as it may sound, Constantine ended up falling for me. It proved to be too little, and much too late. Our own "fifty shades of black."

We had a whole year, happily in love. He was clean, sober, and appeared to be getting his life together. Things were looking good. With my help, he rebuilt his credit, was able to help his daughter with college, and I even became very friendly with his family. I had never felt this connected with another human in my life. I felt that I had met my soul mate. Together we made a striking couple. People around town referred to us as "Barbie and Ken." We were a presence that would make people stop and stare. It was Constantine that pointed out to me the special something people were noticing, was all me. During our time together, my psychic ability was heightened.

Looking back on our year of bliss, enjoying each other's company as a couple, going out to nightclubs, bars, lovely dinners, private parties—just having a blast, there was something that still wasn't quite right.

It didn't seem to matter where we went, I couldn't shake the feeling that we were being followed by some law enforcement agency. On one such occasion, the police department actually contacted Constantine. He was brought in on suspicion of being a serial killer. A DNA test was issued. He had asked me to accompany him. My suspicions were confirmed when we were told by the police officer that we had been followed on our every date.

Thank the Universe that this was the year that Constantine was behaving himself. My senses were heightened. Every time we were pursued, the hairs on the back of my neck stood on end. I recall thinking to myself, "Thank God the guy is innocent."

During my time with Constantine, my angels were definitely working overtime. At his apartment one evening, while we were hanging out by the computer, he grabbed my waist and pulled me towards him saying, "What if I killed you right now?"

To which I replied, "You and what army?"

Before he could even reply to what I had said, his computer went dark. Power surges are common in Florida, but what happened next was not. His computer rebooted and on the screen appeared a picture of a haunted house with the words "You are dead" scrawled across the screen. Suddenly, a bevy of witches and ghouls appeared. They all had different messages, "Don't touch her" and "Keep away from her". He was spooked. He pushed me away saying angrily, "Get away from me!" I felt his fear. There was no computer program native on his machine that could generate such text and imagery. He turned to me and shouted, "How did you do that?"

I replied, "It wasn't me, it was my angels."

During the course of our relationship, I had gotten to know some of Constantine's friends. They were intent on testing my psychic abilities, so they decided to take me to what was believed to be, by local lore, a real haunted house. Constantine, the ever-fierce individual he pretended to be, decided to wait by the car, in case he needed to call for help, or something. Who was he going to call anyway, "Ghostbusters?" In truth he was scared. His friends and I, on the other hand, had to hop a fence and walk quite a distance before reaching our destination. We came upon an abandoned mansion, riddled with holes. Not a good sign.

I turned to the guys and said, "Whatever happens, don't leave me. I attract ghosts, like moths to light."

We entered the dwelling and I looked down at my cell phone. I saw it was dead, no power. Everyone else's said the same thing.

Dear Reader, *Electronic failure is common in the presence of ghosts or spirits.*

I started to go up the rickety stairs. Something drew me to the room at the top of the landing on the left. When I turned around to tell everyone I realized I was alone. The guys were busy exploring other parts of the house.

The next thing I knew, I felt something grab my ankles and pull, sending me falling flat on my back. I could not see the entity responsible, but I felt myself being dragged toward a hole in the wall. Thank God my hips were too wide to fit. I was screaming at the top of my lungs for my posse to come rescue me.

They found me at the top of the stairs, pulled halfway into a hole in the wall. "What's got you, what's pulling you?" They asked as they grabbed my hands and tried to free me.

I screamed, "I have no idea, just get me the hell out of here." They finally got me out and we all ran. Once safely outside the mansion, one of the guys turned to me and said, "I thought you knew how to handle ghosts?"

I explained, "I could handle one ghost, only there were an additional thirty of them."

His jaw dropped. According to the local legend, the owner of the mansion had invited thirty of his closest friends over for a private party and poisoned them all, including himself, with *Kool-Aid* and vodka drinks.

Not only did they now believe me, but it turned out to be a rather adventurous evening for us all.

Toward the end of an intimate evening with Constantine as we were lying together in bed, the lights in the bedroom blew out, one after the other with a loud boom! Boom! Boom! I turned and said, "Look at what we did, our love is so powerful." I had felt that it was our heavenly connection that caused the psychic fireworks we had just witnessed. Constantine replied, "It's all you, not me."

Years later I realized that our lovemaking made me shine and elevated me to a higher level. All this because I was happy. But with Constantine moments of happiness were brief. I could never be sure of his intentions toward me.

We had just finished watching a movie one night and retired to the bedroom. Both extremely tired, we fell asleep instantly. I woke from my peaceful sleep to the sight of five hideous, bald, miniature demons, atop my body, drawing my breath from me, clawing at my mouth. I was petrified. My breathing was labored and my body was paralyzed with fear. My only thought was how Constantine was not even aware of my struggle when he was lying right next to me. Suddenly, my father's spirit walked through the bedroom door and effortlessly peeled these creatures off my person saying, "Not my daughter, not tonight." My father and my hero. Even in death he was still protecting me.

At that moment, Constantine, turned to me and said, "I thought your father was dead?" Apparently he had been aware of my struggle.

Dear Reader, Constantine was no angel, but he definitely was something supernatural.

At the end of that fantastic year, the dream of a happy life with Constantine began to unravel. I came to terms with the fact that my pseudo-soul mate was a drug addict, and that everything about him was a lie. He was addicted to crack-cocaine, a demanding mistress whose wiles he could not resist.

One night, while out at the local club, Constantine desperately needed to get a hit of something. He wanted an excuse to leave, so he proceeded to pick a fight with me. This was not an uncommon occurrence.

In the parking lot of the club, he turned to me and without warning, punched me hard in the chest. To this date I still have a rib that dislocates because of this. He raised his fist to punch me again, but paused to ask, "So where are your angels now, why aren't they stopping me?"

Just as he was about to lower his arm, a group of guys came rushing over and tackled him to the ground. I simply said, "Here they are."

I got into my car and drove myself home, leaving Constantine to fend for himself and take a taxi. He was lucky it wasn't a police car. Just when you think my nine lives are about to run out, it seems there are nine more.

Though faced with a new reality, I became jealous of this mistress, returned again from his dark past. There was no getting around this lesson, however hard it proved to be. It was one that needed to be learned.

When the relationship finally ended I was destroyed. I had believed the lie that Constantine loved me in return. Though Prince Charming he was not, he pushed me psychically. He seemed to know me better than I knew my own self. This enabled him to misuse my psychic talents for his own advantage. But that which does not kill us, makes us stronger, a motto I adhere to each day of my life.

As our relationship began to deteriorate and the fighting became more pronounced, I believed Jimmy may have been trying to channel his energy through Constantine. It was a means of subduing the otherwise drug-induced rages that turned Constantine into a savage beast. This only served to confuse the issue in the end because I would fall back into believing that Constantine may really be Jimmy. I even believed that should Constantine ever come into harm as a result of his own actions, that Jimmy would assume his body and identity. I was treading on dangerous ground. My thoughts were a battleground for the war being waged between my heart and my head. Both camps being fortified by my own psychic abilities.

In the meantime, our storybook romance started to resemble a page right out of the novella *The Strange Case of Dr. Jekyll and Mr. Hyde* by Robert Louis Stevenson.

At the end of the day I wanted people to know that I was only a girl, or rather, a woman first—able to make mistakes, because of a misguided heart. Up until this point, I had only known my hell with Lucien. Constantine may have told me a lot of lies that I blindly accepted, but he would be no better than Lucien. Except he turned out to be my greatest teacher. And if asked today if I had to choose between Lucien and Constantine, Constantine wins hands down. Under the influence he may have been a monster, but when he was sober he had a heart, whereas Lucien did not. He was pure evil.

For me, the little time I spent with Constantine was liberating. Until that time, my life was lived according to the well-intentioned advice of family and friends. My twelve years with Lucien were stifling.

As a single woman, I was on a journey of self-discovery. During the three years spent with Constantine, he would be my tour guide. This life was not free of sacrifice. I partied hard but never neglected my children or my work. I was burning the candle at both ends. I wasn't sleeping much, or eating well. I was losing a lot of weight and compromising my health.

Yet Constantine challenged me to learn more about myself in the process. He wasn't freaked-out by my abilities. He was fascinated with them. He accepted me for who and what I was. For me this was like discovering an angel, gift-wrapped straight from heaven. I always had trouble with the men in my life accepting my psychic ability without being threatened by it. Constantine was the first to accept, and even love it. This made me feel special.

However much Constantine helped me come into my own as an individual, I knew in my heart the relationship was quickly starting to fall apart when he had begun using again.

Though I loved Constantine, there was always room to question his motives, and even more so when he was using. There came a time when Constantine had asked me to buy a home with him, assuring me that I need not worry because everything would be in my name. We went as far as drawing up contracts with the homeowners when I realized that I had doubts about the whole situation. I had a major panic attack thinking about having to pay the mortgage on my own because Constantine would bail. It was a very real premonition for me. When we discussed this, Constantine turned to me and said, "Why would you let me take this con so far, if you knew what I was doing?"

I replied, "Why would you even con someone you love?" Hanging out one night, I was the designated driver because Constantine had no license, and he was often out of his mind on drugs or alcohol. I did not like to drive, especially at night because of my poor vision.

On this one night, while driving back to his apartment, he turns to me and says, "You don't realize how gifted you are." I thought to myself, "If only he knew how nervous I get before each reading constantly thinking, what if I don't see anything? What if I just can't do it?"

Constantine was six feet tall and built like a brick; muscles on top of muscles, to my demure, five foot two-inch frame. He would often tell me I needed to step outside of my own box. He proceeded to place his hand over my eyes while I was driving, forcing my head back into the headrest, and said, "Drive! And use only your psychic abilities."

Although I was terrified, I thought, "He's not going to let the car crash because he's in it." I just allowed myself to let go, and let God. I drove a full twenty minutes back to his apartment with only my psychic ability as my GPS and my keen sense of hearing to respond to the occasional direction from Constantine telling me to stop, turn, etc.

He talked me through it. I even parked the car perfectly, next to three other vehicles. I remembered thinking I have trouble doing this in daylight with my eyes wide open. Parallel parking is not even an option. As crazy as that night may have been, I learned to place more faith in myself and my abilities. He taught me to be confident.

Haven't we all dated a Constantine? Maybe not as psycho but we have all had our brush with bad. Somehow there is always something exciting or alluring about dating the bad boy. Fortunately, (that is, if we are lucky) we walk away, realizing that all they are is bad and at times even dangerous. Some women however aren't that lucky, and the price they pay for their adventure is very often with their own lives.

Just before our last big fight, I stayed over at Constantine's. It was Lucien's weekend to have the girls. I recall being awakened by Constantine in the middle of the night.

It was one of the coldest nights that February. I was wearing my blue flannel pajamas with little green frogs on them. He woke me, (and that was no small feat because without coffee to coax me, it is almost next to impossible to wake me), to tell me that he needed to go to his friend's house because he had forgotten his cell phone there and he was expecting a very important phone call.

It was a dark, moonless night and I didn't have my glasses with me. We got into the car and drove off. Constantine directed me while I was half-asleep, exhausted, and in my pj's, until we pulled up to his friend's house. Constantine went in and I waited in the car. He reappeared ten minutes later. He asked me to come in with him because "they," Constantine's so-called friends, wanted to make sure I was not, in fact a cop.

Reluctantly, I followed Constantine into the dwelling. One of the guys said to me, "Lift up your shirt, we need to see if you are wearing a wire."

Before I had time to object, one guy was holding me from behind and the other was pulling up my pajama top, exposing my chest to all those present.

I was able to free one of my arms long enough to punch my captor in the face. This so-called friend was clearly just a drug dealer. He put a gun to my head, and asked, "Who the hell do you think you are?"

I replied, "Who the hell do you think you are, lifting my shirt up like that?"

The guy pushed me into Constantine saying, "I like her." He gave Constantine the drugs he came for, but I noticed that no money was exchanged. The dealer turned to Constantine and said, "We'll talk later."

When Constantine and I returned to the apartment, the drug dealer had called him. "Send her back, I'll take her for payment." I had enough. I got into my car and left. Constantine actually believed that I was going back to give myself up as payment to his dealer. I went home instead. After all that I had been through that night, the last thing I wanted to do was stick around watching my boyfriend get high.

I thought I had finally closed that chapter in my life. I was ready to move on but Constantine was relentless in his attempts to win me back. He finally convinced me by saying he had given up the drugs, and as a celebration he wanted to take me out to dinner. I should have known better. He told me to put on my prettiest dress and directed me to pick him up at a parking lot not far from where he worked. He had mentioned he had to run a few errands and would meet me there. When I arrived at the parking lot, I was surprised to see a group of people, instead of just Constantine. As I got closer, I realized that it was the drug dealer. I was to be payment for a debt owed. I turned to the drug dealer and said, "No way! Nobody owns me."

He put a gun to my head, thinking he could intimidate me. Instead, I told him, "You had better shoot me more than once, and make sure that I am dead, and get the money from Constantine."

He stood there, so stunned by my brazenness that he did not shoot, and watched me turn and walk away. Looking back, I don't know whether it was bravery or stupidity. I only knew that guy was not going to touch me.

When life with Constantine was good it was really great. Constantine had a romantic streak. I recall when he had given me a tanzanite ring. On one occasion when he got mad, he ripped the ring off my finger and threw it out the car window as we were driving. I started to cry and said, "I loved that ring. It was the only thing that you have given me that I really loved."

Constantine had taken what I said to heart. Later that same night he went back to where he had thrown the ring and found it. The next day he gave it back to me.

Throwing what was left of my good judgment out the window, I agreed to spend one last weekend at Constantine's apartment. On that Monday, Constantine was scheduled to appear in court on drug charges. He was afraid of a conviction, so he started doing drugs, the rational solution, and decided to hold me captive.

After about four hours of a drug-induced tantrum, screaming and calling me every name in the book, he started to glow! He became really calm and glowed as if he were a candle. It was like an angel had entered his body. Dr. Jekyll, turned into Mr. Hyde, and he proceeded to compliment me. No one had ever spoken to me in such a manner. I had a scar on my stomach from my spleen surgery which was about ten inches long and looked as if I had received a partial calling card from Zorro. It had always bothered me and made me feel unattractive. Under whatever this influence was, Constantine said, "Your scar only makes you more beautiful because you survived. You are a miracle."

He continued saying, "The light inside you draws me in and makes me feel alive."

He believed that I could cure him of all his ills. He made me feel wonderful. No one has ever made me feel as he did. He was the first person who believed that I truly had a gift. And then, the glow about his person began to fade. It got darker, and darker, until he had a red cast about him, as if he were the devil incarnate.

In the next instant, he turned to me and said, "Don't believe a word of what that guy said. He's a con and a liar, and he's gone."

And suddenly I was being beaten to the barrage of vulgarities flowing freely from the sewer that was now Constantine's mouth. I was scared to death. He punched my face and chest. I had become the receptacle for his anger. With each punch, he would shout out the name of a man that had wronged him.

"Bill you bastard, you owe me money!" "Frank you mother-fucker, you stole my car!"

I screamed helplessly, "Constantine, it's me, it's Tracy!" Miraculously the phone rang, bringing him out of his drug-induced, psychotic state, long enough to answer it.

I couldn't help but believe the phone call was yet another act of divine intervention by my angels. It bought me more time however things were far from over. This would turn out to be one of the longest nights of my life. I kept wondering how much time I had left to live.

After the phone call, he returned his attention to me. He picked up a picture of the two of us together, staring intently at it, and said, "I want your fucking light."

He smashed the picture, picked up a shard of glass, and said, "I am going to slit your throat, and take your light."

I felt at that moment that I was going to die. And then the phone rang again, always at the right time. The shard of glass would be dangerously close to my throat and mutual friends' of ours would call to ask him something stupid, and manage to change Constantine's thoughts in the process. God forbid he didn't pick up a phone call. He was glued to it, and I was grateful.

I had an army of angels on call that night. Literally. Returning from his phone call, he grabbed me by the hair, and said, "You are disgusting and dirty."

By now I am covered in my own blood, and beyond being afraid. Constantine ordered me to get into the shower yelling, "You dirty whore!" He ended up throwing me into an ice-cold shower, in the middle of a very cold Floridian night, fully clothed.

He returned to the sad scene with a razor blade in his hand, turned off the bathroom light, and joined me, fully clothed, in the shower.

He turned to me and said, "If I slit your throat in cold water, you won't feel it."

I screamed at him, "So do it!"

A little startled by my response he asked, "What?"

I continued shouting, "I'd rather be dead, than tortured by the likes of you. You will never get my light. God owns my soul, it belongs to him!"

Constantine started laughing, hugged me, and asks in his sweetest voice, "I thought you were afraid of the dark?"

It was as crazy as it sounds. We left the bathroom. I was exhausted, feeling as if I had taken a long trip to hell and back, when my thoughts were interrupted by a knock at the door.

Constantine ordered me to go and iron his clothes for his court date the next morning. Then he turned and headed for the door.

I could hear my mother yelling on the other side of the door. She knew something was wrong with me. Meanwhile, I tried to come up with a means to escape. I was smart enough not to have plugged in the iron because I didn't want to get burned by the lunatic in the next room. I was just pretending to iron his clothes. When he rejoined me I told him, "My mother won't go away, unless I go to the door."

He agreed to let me go. I said to him, "My mother needs some help with her car, I'll be right back."

I took off like a shot and my mother and I made a successful get-away. I wondered how my mother knew to come when she did. She must have received my psychic 911. She told me that she felt compelled to come and somehow knew I was in danger.

The injuries I incurred that night took a total of two months to heal. Constantine had no recollection of what he had done. I told people a story that I had been hit by a car, too embarrassed to tell the truth. Constantine had beaten me so hard and leaving me in a weakened state, that not long thereafter I became very ill. I was laid up for six weeks in a semi-conscious state with high fevers, causing me to have visions. They could have been delusions except they turned out to be very true.

During one of these visions, I astral-projected to the house I was taken to by Constantine previously on one of his drug deals.

I assumed the image of a male S.W.A.T. team member. I looked down at myself and saw, instead of my petite frame, the body of an extremely well built marine–type figure. I could almost feel my own muscles ripple. I watched myself kick down the door and saw the drug dealer who offered to buy me. I proceeded to kick the shit out of this man. I arrested him and brought him in on federal charges. There is justice in this world after all.

I regained consciousness, called Constantine, and related to him all of my adventures in my semi-conscious state. Constantine seemed to have been stunned into silence on the other end of the phone. He proceeded to tell me that everything I had just related to him was true. He pointed out the exploits of one S.W.A.T. team member in particular. He was rather large and out for vengeance.

Apparently my so-called out-of-body experience was happening in real time! The drug dealer ended up in jail for many years.

One of Constantine's famous lines was, "First time a victim, second time a volunteer."

I was never a volunteer. I was a victim of my heart's poor judgment. In the end, my head won out. I found the strength to send Constantine packing and out of my life once and for all.

As a result of all my experiences with Constantine I have been able to help so many people. I am an empath. I feel other's pain. My magic comes from my ability to turn such nightmarish events into blessings, tools I use to continue to grow and evolve into the human being I am meant to be, or rather, who I already am and yet to become.

On that note, here's a funny story. Our relationship was over, or so I thought. Constantine was like a piece of chewing gum, if you happened to step on it, the gum gets stuck to the bottom of your shoe becoming a sticky mess that is difficult to get rid of. While I had moved on, he moved deeper and deeper into his drug addiction. At the time I was living with my mother and my two daughters who, thankfully, were at their father's on this particular night.

At about two in the morning, the doorbell began to ring incessantly. I answered the door, a little alarmed to find Constantine at my doorstep in a rage. He began demanding that I give him my car keys. I immediately realized I needed to come up with an excuse, and fast. I knew he did not have a driver's license, and in addition to that small fact he was in no condition to drive. I offered to get dressed and take him wherever he needed to go. Thinking ahead as I always do, I saw this as a means for me to get this maniac far away from my mother, and my home.

We were driving in the car, a very nice Volvo I might add, which may have been part of the reason as to why Constantine even dated me. He must have figured that if I could afford a Volvo I must have some money. In reality I got the car used as a result of a divorce in the family.

We were not even five minutes away from the house when he informed me he wanted to sell my car and use the money for drugs. He became very insistent in his demands, shouting at me to give him the keys.

I replied, "Over my dead body."

His response was a little too quick and easy as he said, "Okay!" In the next second Constantine grabbed the wheel of the car and forced me to turn down a side street. "Tonight is the night that you are going to die bitch."

He proceeded to grab my throat and force me down between the two front seats. I had a vision of dying that night. It put fear in me and gave me the strength to fight back even harder. I yanked myself free but I was not fast enough. Constantine grabbed a fistful of my hair. I managed to regain control of the car, turned it around, and started back onto the main street while Constantine maintained a firm grip on my hair.

Once I got back to the main road I hit the door handle and threw myself out of the moving car, into the oncoming traffic. It was like a scene from a movie. I was risking life and limb in an attempt to escape the crazed animal in my car. The oncoming traffic was speeding past me as I frantically waved my hands trying to get someone, anyone, to stop and rescue me. In the midst of this pandemonium, Constantine began driving my car in tight, dizzying circles around me, trapping me in this unbelievable situation.

I was getting tired and beginning to lose my breath. In a desperate, last ditch effort to get someone to stop I threw my body in front of a car and landed on the unsuspecting soul's windshield. I slid across the hood of the car and landed on my feet. I began pounding on the passenger side window, begging to be let inside to safety. No angel, Charlie's or otherwise, could have managed this.

Breathless from my efforts and barely able to utter a word I began to point from the guy I stopped in the car, to Constantine. In a split second he asked me, "Does he have a gun?" I shook my head no. The man let me into his car and set off.

Now safe in this stranger's car, I surveyed my surroundings. My hero turned out to be a computer geek, with computers and parts filling every available inch of space in his car. There was barely any room for me to sit. But I wasn't complaining. The man turned to me and said, "I will drive you to the nearest 7-Eleven and we will call the police."

I could only nod my agreement. I was beyond exhausted and still trying to catch my breath. My heart was pounding hard against my chest and everything around me was moving in slow motion.

We arrived at the 7-Eleven and the man called the police as promised, relaying the events that had transpired. Just as he was going to give them the address to the 7-Eleven, I grabbed his arm and said, "Tell them to go back to my house instead, he's headed back there."

The police arrived at my house to find my Volvo parked in the driveway with the keys inside but no sign of Constantine. They searched the neighborhood but were unable to find him.

The mystery man never even questioned the change in plan. He took off faster than a speeding bullet. Clark Kent he was not, as he left me stranded at the 7-Eleven to fend for myself. I wonder if he would have volunteered to stop if I hadn't thrown myself onto his car. It makes one wonder about people today. The length that one has to go in order to get a helping hand.

I called the two people I knew I could count on, the neighbors that had always been there for me, my real heroes. Stephanie and Gene were the type of neighbors that one would pay extra to live next door to.

Back at home, Constantine called me about an hour after the police had left and said, "I'm not done with you." He had plenty of time to think things over that night on his long walk home.

Tracy

Chapter Eleven

Who Wants to Date a Psychic?

"...he had a way of taking your hand which made
it clear he'd have to be the one to let go."
—Alice Hoffman, "Local Girls"

D ating is hard for the average girl. We all try so hard to find a
compatible mate. Most of us are searching for someone with
characteristics like good looks, success, great family values, and
someone that accepts us. Accepting who I am includes accepting
my psychic abilities and this has been the most difficult part. As you
recall, I was married for twelve years. And each one of them was a
challenge.

It has always been the same scenario; I meet a guy, we click on a
physical level, I tell him I'm psychic, I think he thinks I am making
it up, and then once he finds out how good I am he wants to control
me. "Make me money," "Read my family," or "Talk to my dead
relatives." It usually goes south from there. I would read them at the
end of a busy workday, on the house of course, and it is never good
enough. They are the harshest critics and they always demand more.

It was my last reading of the day and I had a date that night. I
told my mother and daughter that if I went over the allotted time
to knock on my door. Once I started to read my client, a strange
presence filled my room. I was trying to relate some of the events
that would unfold in her life when I was interrupted by this loud
banging within the walls. I said to the woman that my mother was

supposed to knock if we went over but I knew it was too soon. I continued with the reading. The banging became louder and louder as if a demolition crew had set their wrecking ball free on my walls.

I said to the woman, "I don't know what they are doing out there, but they are making a racket."

With a cold, dead stare the woman looked at me and asked, "What are you?"

I replied, "I am a woman, a psychic, a mother and a daughter." The woman became more and more agitated with every bang. She pursed her lips, and repeated, "What are you?"

I responded rather confused, "What do you mean what am I?" The woman explained that she was a witch, and was annoyed that she could not break my force field.

I laughed, and said, "I didn't even know that I had a force field." The witch gave up and left. The reading was over.

I walked out of the room, found my mother and daughter, and asked them what they had been banging because it sounded like someone was banging on the walls with a sledgehammer. My mother responded with a surprised look upon her face, "What noise? We never even knocked. The time wasn't up. If anything, you got done early."

In retrospect, I could only surmise that the witch was trying to break through my force field, and apparently I overcame. Obi Wan Kenobi would have been proud of this young Jedi. Now, with my force field intact I was more than ready for my evening out and looking forward to my date with Josh.

Fortunately I was having an average night out, no weird stuff—yet! We went to a local club for drinks and a little dancing. By the end of the evening, the weather had made a turn for the worst. It was thundering and lightning out, but Josh, like a gentleman, was holding my hand. I looked at him and said, "I wish I would just get hit with a little bolt of lightning, to boost my psychic ability."

Dear Reader, Be careful what you wish for, you may just get it.

And then the night was over, and I was happy to get home to bed. I had to get up early because I had a reading the next morning.

The stormy weather was still around. My client that morning was a Native American woman. We sat down, my black cat was sitting on my lap. The lightning was so bad it caused the power in the house to surge and the lights were blinking on and off. Suddenly, there was a loud bang. Lightning had hit the transformer outside my house. The electricity found a conduit in the water running into the house and made its way toward my reading room, finding its next target—me.

As I began reading my client her grandfather appeared in the room. I put my hands up in the air and said to her, "Your grandfather is here. He is a powerful lightening god!" And that was when the lightening hit me.

I was thrown into the air. My cat seemed to pop like popcorn off my lap. The power surging through me found its way out my right arm. I was terrified, so much so that I jumped onto my client's lap and clasped my arms tightly around her neck. By now the power was out but my client was enthralled.

"Do it again, do it again! I loved it." I don't know what she was thinking. This was no parlor trick. I remained on her lap for forty-five minutes. I was in shock and she was disappointed. Needless to say, she never returned. I probably didn't make the right decision but I went inside and started to drink. I needed to calm my nerves.

About two weeks went by and one of my neighbors commented on my coloring. "My god you look awful," she said. "Are you feeling okay? You're green like Shrek. You should really go to the doctor."

I heeded her warning and made an appointment to see my doctor. I really did feel like crap. I explained to him that I had been hit by lightning. He yelled at me and checked my pulse, except he couldn't find one. He said that I had probably been in kidney failure for about a week and that would explain my green coloring.

He then asked me, "Who drove you here?"

I said, "I drove myself." He could not believe that I was still lucid. He gave me some antibiotics and sent me home.

Dear Reader, The lightning really did kick my psychic abilities up a notch, if not two.

Sometime later I had a fixer-up blind date. In this case I really did wish I was blind. He was, among other things, a little fatter than I normally liked and needless to say we were not a good match. Since one of my clients fixed us up I thought that their "picker" might be better than mine. He lived in Georgia. Very wealthy, he flew me out to his house for a week. He turned out to be just like all the rest. Although he wined and dined me, he would quiz me on disasters and events that had occurred in his city, "How did this building burn down?" I told him the fire was started by a drunk, back in the 1930s.

"Why is this building vacant?" I said, "Since the fire, it is believed to be haunted."

"Why has this town gone bad?" And I replied, "That is just the bad luck of this economy."

Once he realized what I could do, he said, "I am very wealthy and I can back you."

The only stipulation would be for me to leave my family behind, and come live with him in Georgia. That was not an option. Plus, I didn't even like him. He had so much money and he only viewed me as a means of making even more. On more than one occasion I have been referred to as a cash cow. Do you know what that does to one's self esteem?

I realized quickly the relationship was not going to work I chalked it up to just another guy trying to use me for all the wrong reasons.

This next thing is a "girl thing" and not a "psychic thing" but I think you will appreciate it for all the right reasons. The guy from Georgia came to visit me. I told him that I had a big business meeting so he kindly baby-sat my kids while I went out on a date with a cute guy. (Snap!)

Moving on from Georgia, I was thinking I had at last met Mr. Right or the Boy Wonder. He was ten years younger than me and we got along fantastically. We were driving out to see my friend Laurel and her animals on the preserve. It was about a forty-five minute drive. The boy wonder was exceptionally quiet while driving. All of a sudden and out of nowhere, I turn toward him and say, "If you are hungry let's pull over and I will get you something to eat."

He replied, "I didn't say a word, get out of my head."

"You're thinking extremely loud, and I know you don't have any money, but I have money and I will pay for you." After all, he was driving.

He said, "I am surprised by how good you are, but sometimes you creep me out." Just what every girl wants to hear.

To make a long story short, the boy wonder asked me to read his ex-wife as a favor. That was very awkward to say the least. While struggling with this information, the woman was not only beautiful, but ten years younger than myself.

I got so upset before the reading, while blow drying my hair the chord on the blow dryer snapped in half, still plugged into the wall. There was fire coming out of the wall and on the mouth of the dryer. I threw the blow dryer and chord into the bathtub. I should have been electrocuted and was amazed that I wasn't. After that excitement, I proceeded to go and read the ex-wife.

Note to Reader, If anyone ever needs a wingman, I'm your girl.

The ex-wife had the audacity to ask if she and the boy wonder would ever get back together again. I, being the consummate professional that I am, said no. Which was the truth. I went as far as to tell her she would meet another man and have a daughter with him. But people always try to prove me wrong.

So they did get back together again, which of course meant I was out. They ended up breaking up and she is now with another guy. I never did find out if she got pregnant.

I was with my veterinarian friend at a bar we would frequent regularly, listening to some local band. There was eye candy to be had. I liked the guitarist and she liked the drummer. After a whole summer of flirting, this night was the night they actually came over to talk with us. The first words out of the guitarist's mouth to me were, "What kind of doctor are you?" He continued, "I know she is a vet, what are you?"

I replied that I was a psychic. His reaction was one of disappointment. This should have been a sign that all he cared about was money. But who wouldn't fall for the dreamy guitar-playing musician with long hair? That evening we all went back to his place for cocktails. As the night wore on things seemed to be progressing rather nicely and we retired to his bedroom for more privacy. We were making out on his bed, my head on his pillow, when I suddenly found myself tapping his shoulder, and asking, "Who is the old guy behind you?" He replied, "There is nobody here that I can see, describe him."

I did and he said, "That's my dead grandfather." I asked him rather curiously why he would appear now?

He replied, "You're laying on his pillow." I said, rather jokingly, "Why would you give a psychic a dead man's pillow to lie on?"

Now that our make-out session was rudely interrupted all I did for the rest of that evening was a reading with the guitarist and his dead grandfather. After that, I went home. Though our relationship never advanced to the next level I did make a friend. To this day, he has a new appreciation for psychics and when we do manage to bump into each other he is always very kind.

You would think by this point I would just give up on the whole dating scene, but I desperately wanted to be in a relationship. I was out to dinner with my youngest daughter, Marie, one evening Marie, by the way, has acquired some of my talent and she has the ability to read me. While we were at dinner a guy took notice of me and asked for my number. I agreed to go out with him. No sooner had I said yes, Marie said to me, "I don't like him."

I tried to argue, "You just don't like the fact that he is a biker." "I don't like him for you." Marie said emphatically. But as the saying goes, mother knows best, and I went out with him anyway. Our date included a bike ride and drinks. While we were enjoying our beverages, his phone rang. I asked jokingly, "Is that one of your chicks?"

"No, it's one of yours."

It was Marie. She had gotten his number off the caller ID. She was crying hysterically, as she asked, "Why aren't you answering your phone?"

"I couldn't hear it, it was in my purse."

Marie said to me rather firmly, "Come home right now, I don't like him."

Not wanting to upset her any more than she already was, I excused myself and told my date that my daughter was upset and I needed to go home. I learned that later that evening my date wrecked his motorcycle and ended up in the hospital for three months. In hindsight, I was very grateful to my daughter for her intervention that night.

On yet another one of my nights out, my girlfriend and I were dancing to some reggae music at a local club. Out of nowhere, as is usually the case with me, this guy comes up to me, grabs me at my waist, and flips me around like a Ferris wheel. I guess he never saw the drink in my hand because it was raining vodka and cranberry on that dance floor. After his little trick he offered to buy me another drink. Once back on the dance floor, this dancing maven continued flipping me all around. At one point one of these flips landed my butt, literally, on the bar. This was very convenient since I was ready for another drink. However the bartender admonished me instead.

My dancing partner told me he had belonged to a circus act and his partner was just my size. He knew he would be able to flip me with confidence. I would have settled for a simple, "Hello my name is Matt, would you like to dance?" But he does get points for being unique. He caught my attention and, of course, I agreed to go out with him.

He treated me to a lovely dinner at a fine restaurant. On the way home from the restaurant and back to my place, we were just about to cross the bridge when a police officer pulled us over. As it turned out, my date had no driver's license so the officer asked if I could drive. I said yes. Having poor vision at night, as well as a healthy dose of fear regarding bridges, I proceeded to go across it. When I hit the brakes, I found that there were none. From the passenger seat my date said, "Yeah— I need new breaks." We finally made it over the bridge and as soon as we were out of range of that police officer he took over the driving. I did not see that one coming.

I can go on and on, about date after date, where it seems like my psychic ability is a problem, but in the end, when they realize how good I am, it is usually too late. It seems like I always meet these people at a time in their lives when they are in crisis, needing me only to help them solve their problems. I am beginning to believe that my angels are purposely bringing these men to my attention so I can help them.

It was a Tuesday night and I was actually looking forward to going to the movies. My date arrived, I invited him in, and he noticed the writing on my kitchen walls. He turned to me and asked, "Why would anyone write on their walls?"

"My ex-husband would never let me see a therapist, so this was my own form of therapy. By writing on my kitchen walls, I feel that I have broken down my own inner walls."

I am not sure that he was fully satisfied with my answer but we continued on to the movies. While we were watching "A Beautiful Mind" there was a scene where Russell Crowe's character is writing on a window. Without missing a beat my date turns to me and says, "Crazy is, as crazy does." Needless to say, I never saw him again either.

Although it was difficult to always get to that second date, I was persistent in my search to find the right guy. My girlfriend and I were going to a local club and she was the designated driver. As I was getting into her car, she noticed that I was carrying an extra shirt. She asked me, "What is that shirt for?" I replied, "I had a premonition that I am going to need it."

At the bar, my girlfriend commented that my breasts looked rather perky, and asked me, "What type of bra are you wearing?" As she proceeded to unzip my hoodie, she broke the zipper as she was pulling it down. I quickly held my hoodie against my body, feeling very exposed. In the meantime, a small crowd was forming around me at the bar.

My friend quickly disappeared, returning with the extra shirt and I went to the restroom to change into it. She held court at the bar, explaining to my newly formed fan club that I had predicted the whole event. She told them that I was a psychic. Two guys approached us and asked, "Would you like to accompany us to Sarasota tomorrow to spend the day on our private plane?" My girlfriend thought they were feeding us a line, but I said, "No, he is a pilot with his own plane." We ended up having the time of our lives. And no, there was no second date, but only because they were visiting from another state.

I am no longer so desperate to be in a relationship, I realize now that I want the real thing. After all, somewhere out there my Jimmy is waiting.

Chapter Twelve

Animal Magnetism

> *"If animals could speak, the dog would be a
> blundering outspoken fellow; but the cat would have
> the rare grace of never saying a word too much."*
> —Mark Twain

They say that dogs are man's best friend. I had two beautiful German Shepherds in my life; one was black and white, of a pure line, and the other was black and brown, but a Shepherd- Chow mix. I, like all other psychics, have a very unique bond with animals. And I know many animal lovers can relate when I say we all feel as if our animals are our best friends. Not only do I read people, I also read animals professionally.

One of my regular clients had brought his three dogs in for a reading. I looked at the dogs in order to communicate, and the first thing one of the three dogs said to me was, "How is the bird doing?"

I looked up at Mike and asked, "When did you get a bird?"

"I never got a bird." Mike said.

I looked at the dog, and the dog replied, "The bird that hit the window before we left the house."

Mike's face dropped and a tear came to his eye. "Tell him the bird is okay." Mike could not believe the compassion and understanding that his dog possessed.

One of the other dogs chimed in and said, "I like it when you put the green stuff in my bowl."

I asked Mike, "What green stuff do you put in their bowl?" Mike replied, "Asparagus."

Mike originally came to try to keep his dogs out of the kitchen while he was cooking. He was a big man of about six foot three, and all the dogs were about a pound and a half each. I turned to Mike and took one dog's red leash from his hand. I put it in front of the dogs and told them when the red leash is down on the ground, they cannot cross it. Mike never had a problem with them entering the kitchen again.

Now, one might be impressed with the psychic ability of communicating with animals, but I was personally impressed that these dogs could differentiate between the colors red and green. I was always led to believe that animals were colorblind.

I had a friend who had access to large animals because she worked at a zoo. One day while I was visiting my friend, I went up to the tiger cage and started cooing to the tiger. The giant cat began to prance happily around its cage, then stopped abruptly and lifted its tail, spraying me directly in my face. My friend explained to me that I was turning the tiger on, and this was its way of giving me a compliment. However, we were supposed to attend a party later that evening and I had no time to go home and shower. With no other option, I worked the exotic spray through my hair. My friend did assure me that I smelled like buttered popcorn.

As if this was not bad enough, while attending the outdoor party a bird in a tree above me, who had apparently enjoyed a rather large lunch, suddenly deposited its many gifts upon my head. Although some would say that is good luck, it is purely a matter of opinion. The good sport in me was done.

Years after my divorce from Lucien, I was crushing on a guy who worked at the zoo. The man trained exotic tigers and elephants. He was about five-ten with short, brown hair, mesmerizing green eyes, and a ripped body. There was no six-pack; it was more like a twelve-pack. He was your average outdoor man's man.

Tracy really likes cats.
Photo Courtesy of Octagon Wildlife Sanctuary.

On this particular day while he was working with one of the elephants, I was giving him googly eyes and doing my best to flirt. I must have been putting out quite the animal magnetism because the elephant appeared drawn to me, slowly working his way toward me and away from his trainer. As the elephant began to seductively make eye contact with me, he lifted his trunk and gently wrapped it around my ankle, maintaining eye contact with me the entire time. With its trunk around my ankle, the elephant quickly pulled my feet from under me causing me to land hard on my back. Apparently, he was really a she, and she was making it clear there was room for only one girl in her trainer's life.

When Lucien and I divorced, he had obtained a restraining order on me to keep me from seeing my dog Barney, the Shepherd-Chow mix. He knew how much I had loved that dog. We had gotten Barney in between having Megan and Marie.

It was Valentine's Day and I was waiting for the girls to come home from their weekend at their father's, when suddenly Barney appeared in my living room. I put my arms out to him and said, "Come here boy!" He jumped through my body and soul. It was as if he had downloaded all of his feelings toward me. He assured me in that moment that he knew this was not my fault and that he would love me for all eternity. Not long after, the girls came home and said, "Mommy, we have bad news." I hugged them and said, "I know, Barney died. He just came and said goodbye." Crying, we all hugged each other.

Now there is a magical black cat in my life, and no it isn't a panther, although it looks like a miniature one, who I named "Mookie." He has gotten me through extremely tough times, crazy boyfriends, and has assisted me through multiple readings. In some ways he feels like my significant other. He has been the only man in my life who has been consistent and also a bit of a father figure to my daughters. I will explain.

Mookie is there to tuck the girls in at night and he is the first thing they see when they wake up in the morning. He makes his rounds between the bedrooms throughout the night, keeping watch over the family. On one night, Marie and I arrived home after eleven and we realized the house had been robbed. Marie quickly noticed that Mookie was gone and there was an open window. By the time the police arrived, they could see how upset we were that the cat had gotten out. One of the officers took Marie by the hand, she was probably twelve or thirteen at the time, and proceeded to look for Mookie. Together they found him and brought him home. Mookie repeatedly went back and forth from the front door to the open window, letting us know how the burglars came and went. They supposedly had a key.

After my divorce, when the girls were still young, money was extremely tight. For our entertainment I would put catnip all over the girls and myself, and our cat Mookie would just go crazy, jumping all over us. The girls loved it.

And by the way, Mookie dental flosses every day. I hold up the string of dental floss and floss between his teeth. He will not eat breakfast until we complete this routine.

*Dear Reader, Every dead person **that I talk** to emphasizes how important it is to floss.*

Barney

Chapter Thirteen

Food for Thought

"Ask not what you can do for your
country. Ask what's for lunch."
—Orson Welles

It was a Tuesday evening and I had the night off because my children were at their dad's. I opened a bottle of white wine and began to cook fresh tortellini for dinner By fresh I mean the type you buy from the refrigerated section at the grocery, ready in five minutes. While sipping my wine, I added butter and the seasoning packet to my pasta. I took a bite and it tasted terrible! I called the eight hundred number to complain. The man on the other end of the line said, "We don't put a seasoning pack in our pasta. Do you mean the packet that says *Fresh Pack Do Not Eat?*"

I got out my magnifying glass and struggled to read the small print. "Yes," I replied. "That would be the one."

He asked me how many bites I had taken and what I added to the pasta. I said, "One bite and butter." With a chuckle, he told me I should be okay.

By this time, you think I would have learned to scrutinize more carefully everything I put in my mouth.

I decided to take the girls out for takeout at a neighborhood restaurant one night. Marie ordered her usual chicken fingers and Megan ordered her usual cheeseburger. I decided to have fried zucchini. We were all just a little bit too hungry, so as soon as we hit the car we started chowing down on our dinner. I took a bite of my zucchini and got something caught in my teeth. Because I was driving I handed it to Megan and asked, "What is this?"

Megan started laughing, and said, "It's one of those fake, acrylic fingernails. Quite pretty I might add." At least it was not the finger. But I did not finish my dinner that night just in case the finger was in there. The girls devoured their food and said, "It only happens to you mom." Of course the result was several more months of only home-cooked meals.

One evening when life was busy with after-school activities the convenience of fast food was too tempting. The girls got their usual, chicken nuggets, fries, hamburgers, and drinks. Megan was sitting in the front seat and I was driving. A little wary of handling my own takeout, I begged Megan for a handful of fries. I shoveled the fries into my mouth and just as quickly rolled down the window and spit them out! The fries came out, but the matted hair weave was stuck in my mouth. Gagging now, and still trying to drive, I pulled it from my mouth and threw it out the window. I looked at my daughter and asked, "Are you still going to eat that." Megan replied, "I'm fine, it only happens to you."

One might think I have bad luck but I choose to look at it another way. Psychically, I was protecting my daughters, because it really does only happen to me. Any mother would prefer it that way.

On a lighter note, back in the day when Lucien and I were still dating I was working in the hotel business and was invited by a fellow employee to her wedding. This was a big Jewish shindig. We were sitting at our assigned table with my other co-workers and had just finished a delicious appetizer. Dinner was being served. I had ordered the fish, asparagus and the gray mashed potatoes. The gray mashed potatoes came as a side with every dish. The choices were your usual chicken, fish, or steak and a vegetable of your choice. The whole table was leery of the gray mashed potatoes—but not me! I tasted them and, hey Mikey, I liked them! So I started swapping out my salad and my fish for everybody else's gray mashed potatoes.

My table was only too happy to oblige. When the bride and groom came around, I asked, "What did you put in those delicious gray mashed potatoes?" They replied, "They aren't mashed potatoes, they are cow's brains!" Apparently it is a delicacy. Maybe I should convert because I really did like them.

In comparison to eating a hair weave or fingernails, things were really looking up!

Going back a little further, when I was about six years old my parents took me to Germany to visit my mom's homeland. My mother grew up on a farm that was close to the border of Czechoslovakia, near the Black Forest. While there, I enjoyed some buttercream that, to this day, is the best I have ever had. When they say, "straight from the cow", they were not kidding. They milk the cow, churned it into butter, added fresh eggs from the hen, some sugar, and made the most delicious buttercream anyone could have ever imagined.

While this was being done, I was amusing myself with the bunnies. There were about thirty of them, one fatter than the others. I called this one Helmut. I played with this one all day long. When my uncle came to collect me, he asked, "Which one of these rabbits is your favorite?" As I was hugging Helmut, playing and cuddling with my newfound friend, my uncle grabbed him by the ears and told me to go back to the house, he would meet me there.

That night, the whole family sat down for a lovely dinner. I tried the biscuits with the home-churned butter, and I remembered the delicious buttercream. As I bit into my entree, I said, "This is so delicious, what is it?" My uncle replied, "Helmut the rabbit!"

I am not much of a meat eater these days but who could blame me.

Dear Reader, The angels warned; eat the fruit upon the tree, and all the water you can drink, for one day, these will be extinct.

Chapter Fourteen

Everything You Ever Wanted to Know About Heaven

"I shall pass through this world but once. Any good that I can do, for any kindness that I can show any human being, let me do it now and not defer it. For I shall not pass this way again."
—Stephen Grellet

This is my view of heaven. But how do you fit the idea of heaven into one chapter? How can you describe its glory and magnificence, limited by the words and syntax we use to communicate, in only a few pages? Never the less, my view is based on what I remember from my own near-death experience and what I have encountered in my life with my clients and family. One of the things I am personally blessed with is the ability to talk with my deceased family, whenever I want. I can also connect with the deceased family and friends of my clients and I am grateful to share this gift with them. Through this process, one of the first things I have learned is we all go to heaven and so do our animals.

Now you might ask if animals can become people or vice versa. This can happen temporarily but not for an entire lifetime. In other words, your family dog is always your family dog. However, a favorite relative, like a father or grandmother, may pop in when they want but this only lasts for small amounts of time, maybe an hour or so. The family dog is still your family dog, the bird outside your window is just a bird, but maybe for ten minutes, when its eyes are looking directly into yours, it is Aunt Martha. She is letting you know she is there, and just as suddenly the will that you have been looking for falls from a bookshelf and into your hands. And Aunt Martha's job is done. Spirits have the ability to use animals, other people, and also electrical appliances.

Usually I learn the most when I am reading for someone else. Apparently the dead can read the future better than I can. When I read a client, I usually see three spirit guides with each person I read, one guide each for past, present, and future.

A family member that has previously been in your life usually represents the past. This person could go back several generations but it usually signifies who you are as a person, your core values. Your present guide is generally someone closer to you; a mother, aunt, or cousin who has been born and died during this life. This guide represents what your goals are right now. The future guide is usually an angel or spirit guide who has never been born to the Earth plane. They represent who you can truly become. It is your highest potential. This is how I read but other psychics will read differently.

I believe in reincarnation because I can remember past lives that I have lived. The memories of these lives were obtained with the help of hypnosis. In one of these lives, I was a boy in the civil war. I was not even eighteen. My buddy and I had enlisted together and we made a pact; we get in and we get out together. But we didn't make it. I was stabbed with a bayonet in my stomach. My buddy stayed with me until I died. I do not know whether he made it out alive or not, but I doubt it. The fascinating aspect of this story is, despite the fact I am no history buff in this life, I can accurately describe details of the war, like uniforms of the North and South. This time around I also ended up with the same scar on my stomach, this one from a splenectomy.

Another past life I recalled was when I was an eight-year-old girl living on a farm. I was suffering from polio. Unable to run, walk, or play like other kids my age, I remember sitting by a tree playing with animals. The ducks, squirrels, and rabbits were my companions. I died at the age of eight. In this life, I also seem to have an uncanny relationship with animals, although I don't know if this is related to my psychic abilities or my experiences in that particular life.

In a third life, I was a sorceress in possession of extraordinary powers. I became mad at one particular person and, consequently, destroyed an entire city. In this life, I believe I am repaying those choices I made.

I recently read a college student interested in studying the brain. He turned to me and asked, "How would you describe reincarnation?"

I describe it using an analogy of a lily and a human. The lily grows, blossoms, and then dies. The human being is also born, grows, and finally dies. Both of them return to the soil. The bulb could possibly skip a season but will eventually produce another lily, maybe even two. The same is true with the human. He may choose to skip a lifetime but eventually he will be born again and continue the cycle.

Historically, psychics have long been persecuted by religion. Believe it or not, I am a big fan of the Bible. I believe there are a lot of hidden truths within it, especially the passages that discuss the last baby born from heaven. When this happens, and there are no more souls left in heaven, this will be the end of the world. It is also referred to as the Rapture or the Second Coming. What people may not realize is that science is coming to an age where we can clone a human being. This will be the first baby born without a soul.

When asked if I believe in God the answer would be, "Very much so." I trust that no matter what happens, God has a higher purpose for all human beings. I don't always understand the path He takes, but I trust that it is for the highest good. I am going to steal a line from a Garth Brooks song, *Sometimes I thank God for unanswered prayers.* Sometimes we think we want something that is really not good for us. We have all wished for the guy that turned out to be bad, or the job that went belly up. What I do know is there is a higher plan for all of us, and I do not fear it. But what is going to rock the world is the joining of science and religion.

Science and religion are more similar than they are different. Think of them as identical twins, separated at birth. Science and religion were intended to be together and compliment one another.

However because of politics or some other means, they have existed separately, in ways becoming polar opposites. These differences have left a gap for humanity. We have been forced to see ideas as scientific or religious but neither view can fully satisfy or explain our existence. For example, we see a being that does not fit into any construct we have previously known. Do we look at it through the lens of religion and call it an angel? Or do we take a more scientific perspective and call it an alien?

The time is coming when religion and science will come full circle and rejoice in their differences as well as their mutual desires. People all over the world, of all different religions and scientific backgrounds, are coming to the same conclusions. We are calling ourselves spiritual beings, believing in reincarnation, and a higher power that some may call God. We are also believing in alien life forms on other planets, somewhere in the universe. We are looking outside ourselves. The number one common denominator is once again becoming, "do unto others, as you would want them to do unto you."

I do believe heaven is a very real place, and "limbo" is the waiting room. Most of the people that have passed away in this life are all in limbo. These people, like myself, use reincarnation to become a better soul. So if you ask yourself why the world is over populated right now, it is because so many souls are down here trying to get it right. Including me.

In all the conversations I have had with the dead (and I do not consider myself a medium) the number one thing that I come away with is the transcendent power and message of LOVE. No one ever says how much money they had, or how many businesses they owned. They do not bring up how many people they slept with. All they talk about is whoever meant the most to them in the physical world, whether it was a significant other, loyal business partner, a child or grandchild they adored, or a beloved pet. It really always boils down to love. This is how I see heaven.

Heaven is also all knowing. The few times I can recall being up there I felt like an absolute genius. I long for those days every minute I am on this Earth. Each time I read someone, it is like licking the frosting off of a cupcake. It is just a little taste, a tease, of a most spectacular world. A world we will all enjoy one day.

I can honestly say there should be no fear, only love and joy. I have experienced a lot of death in my life; grandparents, father, cousins, ex-boyfriends, pets and I feel confident in what I believe. Heaven is unique to everyone, depending on his or her life-lessons. If they are more evolved, then they are "higher up" on the proverbial ladder. The bottom line is, it doesn't matter where you are because you will just reincarnate and be that much further along the next time around. We are all on the way up. There is no other choice but to do the work before you and improve your status on that ladder.

When Megan was two years old, she came into my room speaking fluent German. My German was not very good, but I was able to understand enough to know she was asking to be buried in Germany when she died. Now remember, Megan is the reincarnated soul of my cousin Muchie. When Muchie died, her ashes were split between the United States and Germany. In this life, Megan is insisting that her remains be buried in Germany. I started to cry and grabbed my daughter. I said to her, "In this life you are mine, you belong to me." In reality, no one belongs to anyone. But that knowledge does not always make it easier when it comes to those we love most.

On a different but related note, it was the night before Easter, however my children had no formal religious upbringing. Marie, who was around two years old at the time, had crawled into bed between Lucien and me. She awoke around three in the morning on Easter Sunday, sitting straight up in the bed, and said, "He has risen."

We are all born into this life with a certain destiny that we are very much aware of, along with the knowledge of where we came from and who we really are. Within three years of our birth, we begin to forget the reason for our journey. Instead we become caught up in mundane details, focusing on how to read and write and acclimate to this life. But some of us are lucky enough to remember and this allows us to grow faster.

The idea of heaven is unique to each individual soul. We each experience it in a way that it is best suited for us. Regardless, it is beyond our comprehension on this plane. The beauty that exists here is found there, only amplified to a level that exceeds our imagination. Remember the quote, "As above, so below. As within, so without." Heaven is the same as earth, only more magnificent.

Chapter Fifteen

Angel Way or No Way

*"I know that you believe you understand what you think
I said, but I'm not sure you realize that what you heard
is not what I meant."*
—Anonymous

My experiences with my angels are as natural to me as it is for the average person to bend down and pet their dog.

I have come to respect the hierarchy and understand the chain of command, as a child would respect and obey their parent. Like that child who chooses to disobey their parent, a punishment must be exacted and lessons need to be learned in order to obtain a higher good. I was a vey stubborn child.

Remember that last stressful weekend I spent with Constantine? He was facing prison and had a court date on Monday to determine his fate. To alleviate some of his stress, he asked me to spend the weekend with him to try and calm him down. That was the weekend that he tortured me. When I finally escaped with my life, I returned home to the safety of my mother and children, only to come down with an extremely high fever. The weekend had proved to be too much of a strain on me, both mentally and physically and my body just began to shut down. Apparently, I was going into kidney failure.

The angels wanted a meeting and the only way to get one was to shut me down. The next six weeks that followed were filled with periods of unconsciousness caused by an extremely high fever. Thank goodness for my mother and children who nursed me through this nightmare.

During those bouts of unconsciousness, I had visions of what appeared to be biblical events, of God and the Devil going one-on-one with each other. It felt odd having these types of visions since I was not raised with religion. I thought my visions were weird.

The angels forewarned me to stay away from Constantine. I was given a direct order to stay away from him and I completely disobeyed it. Now this was the angels' way of conveying to me how evil he truly was. Psychic ability is a learn-as-you-go experience.

The period of time following my weekend with Constantine was like undergoing six weeks of interrogation. The angels are simple and direct, but cross them, and you will experience the full extent of their fury. It was like trying to walk barefoot on a tightrope, and on one side there is ice and the other side fire. I must follow their instructions exactly. There is no room for deviation from this straight, and very narrow, path.

In addition to Constantine, there was a woman named Tammy, a tarot card reader. Again I was specifically told by my angels to *never* use tarot cards. Tammy would give me a tarot card reading, and ended up scaring me, relating horrible things. I, on the other hand, would give people positive and hopeful readings. I had only hoped to receive one such reading for myself. What I did not understand at the time was by getting a reading from Tammy I was, indirectly, using tarot cards.

I was told from a very young age that psychics could not read themselves. Yet today, not withstanding my fair share of grief and a lot of trial and error, I have acquired the ability to do just that. The angels had always wanted this for me. I was to follow only their instruction because they impart the real law of the universe. They gave me very specific instructions to disregard what I heard on the Earth plane. The only truth was imparted by them. This was harder than it sounds.

The high fever I experienced enabled me to realize that Constantine and Tammy were evil. When I recovered from my fever

I rid myself of both of their presences from my life. It's as hard as having a cancerous tumor removed without the aid of an anesthetic, but in the end I would be victorious. That in itself is the subject for a whole other book.

After Constantine I felt like a bottomless pit of nothingness. I listened to my angels but it felt terrible. Although he may have been evil, it did not change the fact that I did love him. He was gone and I was lonely, but in the end I had learned to always choose the path of my angels. I loved them more.

No more than a few months later I began to derail. I dated a string of worthless men and obtained tarot card readings from other psychics. The child was acting out again.

I was at the Tampa Superbowl when a random man in the stands turned around and spat a peanut shell into my eye. I thought I had contracted pink eye after that but when I treated my eye with the drops for pink eye, it burned like battery acid.

This incident led me to seek out an eye specialist. I learned the peanut shell had cut my cornea. He told me now I had a massive staph infection with blisters in *both* eyes. If I had not been treated that day I would have gone blind. The doctor put soothing drops in my eyes, relieving me of the pain. At the same time everything went black.

"This feels awesome but, I can't see anything, it's all black." The doctor explained to me that he "froze" my eyes. He told me it would be about two months before I regained my sight.

I screamed at him, "I have a business to run, and two children to raise, I am a single mother!"

He retorted, "Blind for two months, or blind for the rest of your life. You choose."

With the help of my mother and children I continued to work, using their eyes. They would answer the phones, book the appointments, and help me do things I took for granted everyday when my sight was intact.

In a moment of weakness I asked my angels, "Why is this happening to me?"

"Because you don't know how to listen. So we are forcing you to rely on your ears, and psychic ability."

As a result they succeeded in giving me my greatest gift ever, I learned to really listen. With every punishment, once the lesson was learned, a reward was given. The reward always far out-weighed the punishment.

I equated it to giving birth; the pain would be the punishment and the child, the reward. On many levels, perhaps not as drastic, we are all taken to task and faced with the repercussions of our own poor judgment. We bring this upon ourselves. But as I always say, "We are human," and I often quote, "To err is human, to forgive is divine." I will dare anyone to try to live up to the expectations of my angels. I have endured enough to know that it is far from easy but worth it, and in the end they are always right. I want to be all that my angels want me to be.

Dear Reader, People want to know what it would be like to be me, the psychic that I am. I am sharing with you my painful journey. This is my career and my life lesson, and I am giving it all that I have. I would not trade it for anything in this world.

At the end of my two months of diligently placing drops into my eyes every couple of hours, my sight was returned as promised. I already had diminished vision in my left eye, and the right eye wasn't much better but when your eyesight is taken away completely you gain an appreciation for what you have. Something is always better than nothing and for this I am extremely grateful.

Just when you think things can't get any worse, there is always another lesson to be learned. And it was not be long before that lesson was learned. During my blindness, Megan brought home head lice. Naturally, I contracted head lice as well. When I treated my hair for the head lice it reacted poorly with my previously bleached hair and I went bald in certain spots. Beauty isn't everything; it's better not to itch than have vermin crawling through your hair. To get the visual,

135

my hair was past my shoulders, sporting seven giant bald spots. I looked like a monster, very much like the dead guy in *Poltergeist II*. With good reason, I chose the G.I. Jane cut until my hair grew back.

It was a few weeks before Christmas, and I was living on my own with the girls. Megan was now fifteen, becoming a young woman and wanting to help me. With the help of my mother, Megan put the Christmas lights on the outside of the house. Not knowing the extension chord had been left outside during a rainstorm the holes of the plug had filled with water. When I went to plug the lights into the extension cord I got electrocuted, again. Each time this happens I must say my psychic abilities improve.

Once I stopped shaking I thanked Megan for making mommy a better psychic, but said maybe we won't do outside lights next time.

On a lighter note, the angels speak to me daily and give me little tests to see if I am truly listening. For instance, I might go to grab a pair of green underwear and they might say, "No, grab the pink ones."

If I don't listen they become adamant. At the end of the day they could care less what color underwear I am wearing, but it is just another exercise in doing what I am told.

My daily jogs are another opportunity that my angels use to communicate with me. I find myself more focused and clear while running. On these runs they often speak to me about things that will transpire in the world or with my family. On one of my runs I was overtaken by a much older gentleman. My first thought was wow, he is so much older than me, but able to run so much faster. In that instant my angels afforded me with a visual of an equilateral triangle, at each peak was written a different letter, A, G, E. Each letter represented the following: Always Growing Evenly, AGE. The angels told me each letter also stood for three different focuses in our lives; family, career, and self. The lesson to be learned was to always give an equal amount of attention to each category and that in turn we would age more gracefully.

In regards to world events, one evening while watching the news, it was mentioned that the icebergs were melting due to global warming. My angels interjected by sharing with me that we could stop the melting by fashioning massive, artificial, icebergs. They would be white in color to deflect the sunlight and keep the other icebergs from melting. Once all the icebergs are gone and the waters begin to heat up it will be too late, our planet is done.

On a more trivial note, my angels are rather helpful in the kitchen. I don't really eat meat, but I do enjoy the flavor of meat in my tomato sauce. My angels suggested that I flavor the sauce using beef jerky, which I can easily remove at the end when the sauce is done. They have given me my best secret ingredient for really good pasta sauce.

Dear Reader, It is the best spaghetti sauce that you will ever have.

Chapter Sixteen

Unusual and Bizarre Readings

> *"The world is full of magic things, patiently*
> *waiting for our senses to grow sharper."*
> —W.B. Yeats

I believe each reading I do is unique in its own way and all are absolutely extraordinary and mind-blowing. For me, the mind-blowing part is that my angels always get it right. I am just the messenger and they never fail to leave me in awe. Some readings are a little bit more unusual than others. Here are a few of the exotic readings.

My mother was dating a gentleman whose wife was still alive. However she had Alzheimer's and was living in an assisted living facility. Because of this situation, their relationship never grew past friendship. As a favor to him I went to the home to read his ailing wife. She was unable to speak and only made vowel-like sounds. She was drooling and didn't seem to be in control of her physical body. When I started reading her telepathically she told me of the home she and her husband shared. She went on to describe the children they had raised together and how happy they once were. The gentleman began to cry and said, "She's still in there." She also spoke of current events and things she needed him to do for her.

The whole time she was leaning on me and licking me, which was a little disgusting. And then I began to cry. The gentleman asked, "Why are you crying?" I said, "It breaks my heart that she is alive and well in there and can't communicate on her own."

Word, or shall I say thought, spread fast in the assisted living facility. As I tried to leave, the residents came toward me. One man wanted his diaper changed, another woman said, "Call my children and tell them to come."

The gentleman said to me, "You have such a gift. You can be rich just reading old folks in assisted living." I replied to the man, "I couldn't do this again, this is breaking my heart." I ran out.

I have recently learned that by placing my left hand over my client's heart, and with my right hand holding their hand, I create a conduit. This allows them to use my body as a means to speak freely, as if they were whole again. Conditions may vary depending on the individual but nine out of ten times it works.

The next story involves one of my youngest clients, a three-year-old boy. He had severe autism and a cleft palette, which made it hard for him to speak. I read him, one on one, and he told me telepathically that he wanted to be an auto engineer just like his dad. He told me that when he grows up his cars will fly.

When I relayed this message to his parents they cheered up and gasped. "Tracy, he rips the wheels off every car we give him, and now we know why."

Another interesting reading also involved a little boy of about six years old. I was doing a benefit in a local mall and this little boy sat down. It was like reading an adult male. He was extremely well educated. I told him that I saw him building movie theaters on the moon. He replied, "I've had that dream as well." I then told him he was going to have a little sister. And he said, "My parents are discussing it as we speak."

For a while I had a steady stream of clients that were hearing impaired. Here is the kicker, they wanted me to read them over the phone. We did this with the help of a translator. I will try just about anything, but what repeatedly happened is the translator would cut in and say, "Nope, that's me, you're reading me." That was when I realized I needed to hear their voice. So I asked the hearing impaired people to make some sounds so that I could get into their energy. Once this was done, I was able to read them.

One of the interesting aspects of my gift is that I tend to feel what the other person is feeling. I guess that is why I am sometimes referred to as a sensitive or empath. This is why I do not allow people to drink more than one drink before I read them, or I will feel tipsy during the reading. On one such occasion I was reading a woman who had just recently become pregnant. The morning sickness was just starting but I was one step ahead of her. I put my head between my legs and said, "Oh God, you have morning sickness." She shortly followed and did the same. We both became so nauseous that I was unable to do the reading.

I called her husband and said, "Neither one of us can drive, please come get your wife." He asked what I did to her. I replied, "What did your wife do to me?" I asked her to come back in three months.

I had a client who had accompanied a few of her friends on their readings before finally requesting a reading of her own. I obliged but the reading took a very unusual turn. I saw a giant mass in the woman's stomach and told her that she needed to go to the doctor. I told her that it was all bunched together, like cobwebs. She got mad at me. "I feel fine, you are making that up."

I didn't blame her. Nobody wants to hear they need surgery. She came back six months later after having surgery to remove the mass. She told me the thing that blew her away was how her doctor had explained the mass. He said it was like a bunch of cobwebs bunched together, just as I had described. She is now one of my most loyal clients.

During a psychic party I was reading a lady that was severely over-weight and quite advanced in age. I told her that she was three months pregnant. She became outraged, she said, "I am over fifty and about a hundred pounds over-weight, are you insane? You're just saying that because I am fat."

She was freaked out to say the least. As it turns out, a couple of months later she called me and said, "You were right, I am pregnant, and I am keeping the baby." Now it was my turn to be blown away. I am always amazed at what my angels decide to share.

A woman had brought her problematic son to me for a reading. He had been in and out of jail because of drugs and she was hoping that I could fix him. He was bipolar and, to my surprise I found him to be evil. While I was reading him I also managed to read his thoughts. He was sitting there scanning the room, looking at objects and trying to figure out how he was going to kill me. He would look at a sharp object and think, *I can stab her with that,* or he would look at a blunt object and think, *I can hit her with that.*

So I had to improvise. I said, "Let me tell you a funny story about a couple of guys that tried to jump and kill me. They stabbed me, and left me with this scar." I then lifted up my shirt and showed him the scar from having my spleen removed. "Sadly those two did not survive. I don't know what prompted me to tell you that story. Oh well, back to your reading."

This cleared my little friend's head up, and all his thoughts of killing me were gone. His mom said that he has actually been better ever since that reading.

One day I did a reading with a man named Charlie. Fast forward six months and I hadn't seen or heard from him since. He was having a conversation with my friend Susan at his home. At the same time, I was on the other side of town, alone in my car, going over a bridge. As I went over it, I hit upon a certain frequency in my head. I could hear the conversation between Susan and Charlie as it was happening in real-time. Charlie was complaining to Susan about how he really didn't think I was a very good psychic because so many things had not yet occurred. When I reached the other side of the bridge, I pulled over and immediately called Susan. I said, "Hand the phone to Charles." I screamed at him, "How dare you talk so badly about me. Give it a little bit more time and everything the angels said will come true." He was white as a ghost as he handed the phone back to Susan, and said, "I'm a believer."

I have been blessed with many clients both here and abroad. One of my clients called me from her home in Paris, explaining she had lost her cat. I told her I knew exactly where her cat was and if she followed my instructions, she would find it. I began telling her that I saw a wrought iron fence covered by very thick shrubbery. It looked like a park of some sort. She knew exactly where I was talking about. I mentioned that she should bring some cat food with her. Before the day was out she called to tell me she found her precious kitty, right where I had told her.

There are so many readings I am amazed and blessed that I have been privileged to be a part of. I would not trade my gift for anything in the world. I have come to realize deep down we are all the same, just wanting to be loved.

Kybar

Chapter Seventeen

Nancy the Ghostwriter

*"When I am writing, I do not distinguish
between the natural and supernatural.
Everything seems real. That is my world, you could say.*
—Haruki Murakami

Back when I first had the idea of writing this book, it was
suggested that I use a ghostwriter. I wanted somebody that
knew me and who better than Nancy. She was one of my first clients
when I started doing readings over twenty years ago and is now one
of my dearest friends. Since I talk to ghosts and see ghosts I believe
it is only fitting that my readers know my ghostwriter.

Nancy and I first met when I lived in New York. She and
her mother were out shopping at a nearby mall, one of the many
distractions they engaged in since her stepfather's passing less than
a year before. Nancy and her mom had been wandering aimlessly
through the mall until they had enough. They decided to leave, taking
their usual route through JC Penny's to their car parked just outside.

On the light pole in front of them was a flyer advertising my
services. Nancy mentioned that it probably had been there all along,
but she and her mother only noticed it as they were getting into the car.
Nancy and her mother arrived simultaneously at the same thought and
both moved from the car and were in front of the flyer in a second flat.

Nancy and her mother, Maria, arrived at my house as Lucien
took the kids for a walk, as was the custom when clients arrived. I

smiled at them, shook their hands, and asked who recommended me. Word of mouth was my only source of advertising. Nancy presented a piece of paper with my number that she had torn from the flyer. I was in shock. I never put up flyers, and it wasn't even in my handwriting.

And now they were here. I figured it was meant to be and decided I should read them. I turned and asked, "Will the gentleman be getting a reading as well?"

They both looked at me, then behind them, and then at me again. In unison they asked, "What gentleman?"

I described him in detail, down to the very clothes he was wearing. They stood frozen before me. Recounting the story later Nancy told me they were shocked, every hair on the back of her neck was standing on end. Staring, Maria said, "That's my husband." At the same time Nancy said, "That's my step-father." And that is why they came to see me.

"Well good. You are all here." And I showed them inside the house. While I was reading Maria, I looked out of the window and noticed a double rainbow in the sky. I said to her, "You have been married twice, there is a rainbow for each one of your husbands." She replied, "Yes, you are correct."

I continued by saying, "But I doubt that you can see it." She turned around to look out the window and said, "Yes I can."

Dear Reader, *More times than not it is difficult for me to discern what is real or just a vision.*

Many years later I moved to Florida but continued to stay in touch with and do readings for Maria and Nancy. When I decided to go back to New York for a visit, Maria graciously gave me the master bedroom to stay in. When I got to the top of the stairs, I bent down and began to pet their cat. I turned to Nancy and asked, "Can I take the cat to bed with me?"

Nancy stood there, frozen again and replied, "Tracy, what cat are you talking about?" I described a black, orange, and white Tabby.

"We put Nikki down six months ago."

"Then I guess you won't mind if I take her to bed with me."

As the years went by and our friendship grew, Nancy, who is also a brilliant artist, offered to paint a mural in my girls' room. I wanted palm trees on the wall that would lean in over my girls' beds. Nancy turned to me as she was looking out the window and said, "Why palm trees, you have them right outside your window?" I was having a "Corona" moment, thinking about palm trees, a hammock, and a beer. After all, I was living in paradise. It was like a working vacation, but fun nonetheless.

Mural in Tracy's daughters' room

Late one night I went into the girls' bedroom and told Nancy I was going to bed.

"Who is the lovely woman joining you with the painting?"

Again I managed to stump Nancy. She turned to me and said, "There is nobody here."

I proceeded to describe an older woman wearing a tailored shirt and skirt. She had an apron around her waist and wore a pearl necklace. On her feet were house slippers with a little bit of a heel.

Nancy gasped. It was her grandmother. "I think that's enough painting for this evening," she said. From that night on, Nancy chose to paint only during daylight hours. Little did she know her grandmother was there the whole time, I just didn't say anything.

We returned to my house one night after spending the evening at some local clubs. Having had one drink too many we got back to the house and I passed out on the living room rug but Nancy still wanted to stay up and watch a little television. I had a couple of remotes on the coffee table and Nancy was asking how to turn on the television. My eyes closed, barely conscious, I directed her, "It's the one to your left. Grab it." Having located the remote Nancy was about to press the wrong button when I yelled, "No, not that button! The yellow one on the left."

Nancy turned around in her chair and asked, "How are you doing this?"

"I don't know," I moaned, never once opening my eyes or stirring from my place on the floor.

A note from Nancy- Tracy will sometimes, when in the company of others, respond to a question that was never said aloud. She so easily navigates between the two states that it is difficult to differentiate between the inaudible thought that enters her mind and someone verbally making a request. If ever in her company, don't be surprised if she answers the question you were only thinking about asking. It may be a little distracting at first but it is never boring. This tendency is stronger with people that she is meant to be in contact with.

It has been a constant struggle for Tracy to prove her abilities. As a result, her personality has been fashioned around this fight for truth. She wants, almost needs, to be believed. Her integrity is very important to her. Tracy's life plays out like a supernatural movie, only she doesn't have the luxury of a script to anticipate what will be around the next corner. It is a real trip hanging out with her. She can suddenly start talking to someone who is not there, and if you don't know her, you would probably think she was crazy. After all these years of friendship I know better but on occasion she may turn to me and say, "Can you believe that guy?" And I will reply, "What guy is that Tracy? I don't see anybody."

It is only then that she realizes and says, "Oops wrong plane!" Can you imagine being on call twenty-four seven, having both spirits and humans asking for help and wanting to have their questions answered? Spirits do not operate between the hours of 9:00 and 5:00. At least humans still need to make an appointment.

On one occasion, I asked her what she did to drown out the constant spiritual banter. How did she ever get any sleep? She mentioned that in the evenings she leaves her television on. When she is going to sleep she convinces herself the voices are coming from the television and not her spirit guides. And sometimes the occasional cocktail or glass of wine is also helpful.

Chapter Eighteen

A Passion For Reading

"In faith there is enough light for those who want to believe and enough shadows to blind those who don't."
—*Blaise Pascal*

Life is not without challenges. Although we may feel alone on this journey, those feelings could not be further from the truth. We are all interconnected and part of something much greater than any individual can begin to imagine.

If we are lucky, we encounter people like Tracy that ease our anxieties and show us the magic this life has to offer. Whether we look forward to the future, or behind at our past, the greatest gift, as they say, is in the present. And it is a present that can be obtained with the exceptional talents of a gifted psychic who works tirelessly to help people find their peace.

Thank you Tracy.

With love, Nancy

September 8, 2011

Tracy Williams is simply one of the most accurate psychics I have ever met. She is a pretty, sweet, down-to-earth person with blond hair and an easy laugh, and you would never expect this unassuming mom to be an extraordinary intuitive —— but she is. My first reading with Tracy was over the phone —— we had never met and I was interviewing her to see if she was gifted enough to be one of the 25 psychics I was inviting to be part of a "Predictions for the New Millennium" press conference in New York. Within a few minutes, Tracy correctly described most of the major events that were going on in my life —— job, relationships, family. She even described my recently deceased father, right down to the color of his hair, how he died and the way he used to joke with me. I hadn't said a word, but Tracy knew me inside and out. I invited her to attend the press conference, which was attended by 75 top media outlets —— including CBS News and the Wall Street Journal —— and received coverage all over the world. Tracy was a standout at the event, wowing even the most skeptical journalists with her accurate readings and predictions for the future.

After that event, Tracy and I became friends. That was interesting, because Tracy "knew" everything about me —— she knew which of my teeth had fillings, how I felt about certain members of my family, how long I would stay in a specific job, which men I would date, when I would marry and how many children I'd have. Sometimes, I didn't like what I heard. Once, after I took a high- profile, global PR job with a major corporation, I told Tracy that I was planning to buy a house near the corporation and relocate. Even though I was excited about being in this new job, Tracy said "Don't unpack your boxes —— this job isn't going to last, in fact, this company might not last." I was disappointed and wanted to doubt Tracy, because this was a thriving company and I couldn't believe that it would fail —— but she had been right so many times in the past that I decided to rent an apartment in the area instead of buying a house. Within a year after I was hired, the company was bought by a rival company and most of my former colleagues lost their jobs. I say former, because I left the company in advance of the buyout. Once again Tracy was right —— even when every logical thing pointed in the other direction.

Sometimes Tracy would amaze me with simple, day-to-day predictions. One afternoon, we were chatting on the phone and I told her that I was really annoyed because I had lost my day planner when I had traveled from New York to Pennsylvania the day before. I had no idea were I'd left it —— in the cab, plane, airline lounge? —— But all my notes, phone numbers and more was in that book, and I hadn't even written my name and contact information in it, which would have been handy if I ever misplaced it. "It's in California. You'll get a phone call within four days from someone who'll tell you they found it," she said. I told Tracy that I thought that was unlikely because my phone number wasn't in the book, but she stuck to her prediction. I thanked her but privately didn't get my hopes up, because I didn't really believe that what she said was possible.

Three days later, on a Sunday night, I got a phone call. It was a supervisor in the lost and found department of U.S. Airways. "We found your day planner," he said. "It was left on the plane that departed from the Pittsburgh airport a few days ago —— we'll send it to you." I asked the man how they tracked me down when there were 365 pages of notes about people I'd met and projects I was working on but no contact information about me. Apparently, the man had looked through the book and saw a note I made —— sometime in September —— about my new U.S. Airways frequent flyer number —— I must have scribbled it down for some reason. I thanked him and asked if he was calling from the Pittsburgh office of U.S. Airways. "No," he said. "I'm in our California office —— the plane you left it on departed from Pittsburgh to California a few days ago."

I could go on and on about Tracy and her phenomenal psychic ability —— but there are too many stories to tell. I will say that I have interviewed hundreds of psychics for a book that I'm writing, and Tracy's laser-beam ability makes her stand out as one of the best. She is also a tremendously nice, caring person, and her reputation as one of the most gifted intuitives in the country is truly well deserved.

Mary Ann

Hi Tracy,

In 2008 my husband put his house up for sale in Rochester, New York during a rough time in the housing market. We live full time in Los Angeles now, so the distant financial responsibility was starting to take its toll. We completed essential fix up projects, tagged the house, and garnered the service of a Real Estate agent known in the family for years to handle showings. After several months of the house being on the market with no signs of a sale, both the Real Estate agent and my husband's parents (who co-owned the home) were ready to take down the listing, board up the windows and try again in the spring. During a reading with Tracy, she said that the house would sell in a few weeks and that we should keep it up for sale. I begged my relatives to keep an open mind and let the right buyers find the house. I urged them to keep the for sale sign up to continue to host open houses. As predicted, within 2 weeks of Tracy's reading, the perfect buyers (with cash!) bought the house and have been free of that stress ever since.

Tracy's readings really seem to be on target and have been very helpful to me and my family. Last year she predicted a normal pregnancy for me, even after my own gynecologist and many statistics stated the chances of being fertile were very slim because of my advanced maternal age of 43. Tracy's reading gave me the confidence to go ahead and try to get pregnant in the first place I was fortunate enough to get pregnant quickly and naturally, without having to receive fertility treatments. We are now enjoying our healthy, happy little girl. I will continue to consult with Tracy for input on pivotal decisions in the future. She's the real deal!

Shelly from Los Angeles

January 14, 2011

When our house was for sale in Maine I called Tracy to see when it would sell and by which agent. I asked would our agent Tim sell the house Tracy said No it will be a pretty blonde lady to sell the house and a single woman buying the house. Our home was shown lots of times and the agents left their cards. We would always look to see if it was a blonde lady on the Real Estate card. The Agent that showed our home and presented am offer did not leave a card so we didn't know what she looked like till closing. Of course she was a pretty blonde lady and the buyer was a single woman.

Sue
A friend in Naples, FL

It is an honor for me to be able to brag about my sweet, sweet Tracy! We are both eleven babies, meaning we were born on the eleventh day, but of different months. When I first met Tracy I felt an instant connection. She is amazing, bright, refreshing spirit. Her presence gives me a warm sense of reassurance. In my last reading with her she predicted that I would meet an amazing man, and other things that have since come true. I would have never guessed in a million years it would be her gorgeous cousin. She is my angel, she is my butterfly and I cherish the time we spend together. The world is definitely a more beautiful, peaceful place with her in it.

Elsa Puerto

April 15, 2009

Thank you again for helping me. You continue to give me insight that is truly remarkable. My daughter was very disbelieving when I told her last year that she would become a mother. She really had given up. She stopped taking her birth control pills when she graduated from Dental School. That was 19 years ago.

She is pregnant and due on June 21st (Fathers Day), and she will be having a girl just like you said!

Highest regards to you,
Jan Morgan, Family Nurse Practitioner, Hood sport, WA

Tracy's insights and intuition are spot on. Having worked with her for the past several years, I've been able to make informed and confident decisions in both my business affairs and in my relationships, based on her readings.

Tracy's acute insights were most appreciated last year when she was able to intuit that the business partner I was about to select was not so sound of mind. Months later we saw several examples that proved her prediction was right and I was most grateful not to be associated with this person in business.

Most recently, Tracy predicted that a former relationship (which I thought was completely over) was to resurface again. Having this foresight allowed me to prepare mentally and emotionally, thus preventing me from getting pulled back into old, unhealthy habits from the past.

Tracy provides an awareness which allows her clients to make wise, informed decisions, to uncover underlying reasons for stress, as well as work through issues that affect their overall well-being. Working with Tracy has allowed me to maintain a healthy and balanced lifestyle.

Kelly K Florida

Dear Tracy,

For the magical reading, for sharing your gift, and your immense talent, for opening yourself as widely as you did to look deeply inside my soul, I extend my gratitude...

Since you often use the stones of those who seek your guidance, I wanted you to have one of my favorites, it is a manifestation piece, I kept it beside a rose quartz all of these months, as I healed from what transpired in Italy, half of my quartz remained with my karmic lover, across the romantic sea, the relation so far behind me now, I realized after our reading that my half of the rose quartz was to be discarded, as the self love it generated which once melded with his half, this along with the manifestation stone I kept beside it, they completed their joint work in helping me manifest the future that is about to become my present, and so, the manifestation stone is now yours, to use to help others do the same....

I look forward to meeting with your energy again and again, as we look into what is before me, together, and explore all the wonder ahead!!!!

Warmly, Lisa Bernhard

"Tracy predicted I would meet the love of my life more than six months prior to that happening! She even described the dimple in his chin – amazing!"

In love in Washington

Tracy has been so inspirational in our lives. She has been reading for me since 2005. On many occasions when my life has been turned upside down she has always been there to pick me back up. My husband lost his job 16 months ago when things just didn't seem to get better I called Tracy and had her read for me. Things started happening just like she said they would. She is very accurate. She got me thru 4 years of my son serving in Iraq and much more. I don't know what I would have done without her.

Joann Connell

June 15, 2010

Tracy,

I just wanted to send you a little token of my appreciation. I know that this is your business, but I feel that we have and are continuing to form a friendship.

I appreciate the way you take the time to talk and explain things from a different view (angle).

I know that God has blessed you with a gift and that he only allows you to see what he wants you to see and that you don't have all the answers. Praying and waiting on God is SO hard sometimes. Our lives also can get at a standstill which can drive you crazy.

I hope that you like it.
Thanks again for just being you.

Casandra

During the course of my divorce, Tracy offered me tremendous support and guidance. There were many times when I became weak and was ready to throw in the towel, but she kept insisting it would only be a few more weeks. Now understand it had been almost 3 years so how could she be so sure it would only be a few more weeks. She insisted mediation would take place in May and the divorce would be finalized in June.....for the record, my mediation was May 19 and my divorce was finalized June 13. Glad I listened. Over the next few months I struggled with understanding many things, but again, Tracy's support was unfaltering. I was informed at the end of the year by my children that my ex was getting remarried. My first thought of course was that his future wife was pregnant. I called and I met with Tracy and she insisted this was not the case. A month later they announced that the new bride was in fact pregnant. I naturally called on Tracy to let her know and she was silent for a moment and insisted something was wrong and there must be more to the story. She kept telling me, that this woman was not having a baby; in fact she went so far to say that she would never have children. Less than 2 months later, I heard my former sister in law that my ex-husbands wife miscarried and then had a hysterectomy. As sad and tragic as this was for them, it was exactly what Tracy had predicted to be the case. It takes a confident person in their gift to argue something so strongly knowing that it was completely contradictory to what was known to be a fact at the time. Tracy is a wonderful, caring person who will go out of her way to be helpful and understanding and she is blessed with an amazing gift.

Thank you, Jen

My name is Ann Williams; I'm Tracy's mom. I was born in Germany, and I came to America when I was seventeen. My husband Bill, and I had two children; a girl named Tracy, and a boy named Jack. When I was in Germany I had never heard of a psychic. When Tracy was thirteen years old she flew to California to visit her Aunt Barbara. Aunt Barbara picked her up from the airport and she said, "Let's go take a look at Uncle Bob's new office." Tracy replied, "I already know what it looked like." Barbara was shocked! She said, "How do you know? You've never been to California." This was my first experience that Tracy was psychic. I wasn't surprised, because my mother-in-law also claimed to be psychic. Over the years, Tracy predicted many things, from death, to minor details. Many years later, when my grandchildren were little, we took a trip to Disney. At that time it was my husband's fifty-sixth birthday. Tracy gasped, and said, "Oh my gosh, I see him dying at fifty-eight." I replied in disbelief, "How do you know? You're not God." I put it out of my head, and I never thought about it. A year after this incident, my husband was diagnosed with bladder cancer, then shortly after, bone cancer. I never thought that he would die from this. Three months before he died, the doctors informed us that he was terminally ill. Bill died three days after his fifty-eighth birthday. At this point I knew Tracy was right, she was a real psychic. While on his deathbed, he pleaded to Tracy to "cross him over." Tracy exclaimed, that if he doesn't let go of her hand, to split them apart, because he would take Tracy over with him. I did have to do this. It certainly gave me a new perspective on life, and on Tracy. To this day, I consult with Tracy before I do anything.

Anna Williams

My name is Marie; and I am Tracy's youngest daughter. Growing up with a mother as a psychic was very difficult for me. In elementary school some of the sophomoric kids would taunt me about my mother's abilities. I told them she was a psychic, and they would reply, "NO, she's a psycho!" This response always made me feel dejected and uncomfortable. The kids challenged me, and said, "If she is really a psychic, run away and see if she finds you." Wanting to prove my point, I did just that. Back then, "running away," to me, meant hiding behind an orange tree in the backyard. Kneeling in the dirt, I kept saying in my mind "find me, find me, find me," and not surprised my mother did. I told the kids at school, and of course they didn't believe me, but I had enough proof to suffice. Nowadays, everyone who knows my mother's profession thinks it's mind-boggling! My friends are always asking for readings. There definitely are pros and cons of having a mom who is psychic, but if I had a choice, I wouldn't change anything. I've grown to accept her god-sent abilities, and I see my mom as a prodigy. I love her so much, and support her 100% in anything that she does.

Marie

June 1, 2008
Re: Tracy Williams

Dear Ms. Figueiredo—

I hope I am not too late to give her tribute in her new book.

I first met Tracy 14 years ago when a close friend of ours was murdered. She had offered to help, and through her psychic ability, we were able to find out who, and what happened. Since then, she's been my friend and mentor.

One psychic incident occurred when I had asked her to come to my home to give a reading of the spirits residing there. She had told me ahead of time to unplug T.V., stereo, etc. I didn't understand at the time, so I didn't do it. When she came, and her ability was wide open for the reading, she blew out our stereo like she threw water on it. Of course after that, is she said to unplug something, I did it!

As a psychic I trust her to the universe.

As a woman and friend, I would trust her with my life. Her gentle ways and kind actions, give her an aura of goodness.

She is my friend and I am proud to know her as a human being.

Affectionately, Kyle L. Pepin nc

Tracy,

If I could pinpoint a moment in my life where I hit a major life transformation, it would be the moment that I met and received a reading from you. Your reading inspired me to become someone better than I thought I could ever become. Your readings are truly empowering. It was like I had been sleeping my whole life and your reading awakened my soul. I have not only been blessed to see these amazing changes in myself, but in others that I have referred to you. I have witnessed the strength and the courage that you instill in others by your spiritual guidance. You have affected so many lives and I for one owe you gratitude. Thank you!

Zulma M. Raffo, LMSW, PhD

From: Cici Carter
To: Tracy Williams
Subject: Testimonial From Cici Carter
Date: Sat, 16 Aug 2008

Tracy Williams is a visionary and a great one at that. Her psychic abilities are outstanding. Her readings are accurate and the events are unfolding on a continuous basis. The timing is one of the Universe, however, what she reads continues to happen daily. She told me about my job, my business with Delta Duty Free, its success and the popularity that has occurred. She saw sculptures with my jewelry and now I have recreated Anthony Quinn's Sculptures into a jewelry line named Anthony Quinn Jewels. Anthony Quinn is the two time Academy Award winning actor and artist. I had the pleasure of meeting his wife in London during the same time that Christies of London was auctioning my jewelry for their charity Aids Foundation. It is amazing what she can see and how wonderful a human being she is. I recommend her to everyone, her kindness and compassion is remarkable. All the best to you Tracy!

Love Cici Carter

My story of Tracy Williams:

It was the summer of 1999 when I first met Tracy Williams. At the time I worked at a small airport in Florida. I had heard about Tracy and told several of the people in the office. We were like a small family so we decided to take a road trip to Fort Myers to get individual readings. What amazed me was as each person returned from their reading they were far from generic as most psychic readings are but instead were as individual and detailed as each person's DNA.

As we gathered at the bar around the corner from Tracy's home awaiting for the hour of our reading my boss approached me after his reading. He asked me if I had told her about his family. The funny thing is I had never met his family, they lived up north. Tracy told him that his father had a prosthesis and was missing a leg. His sister had been a dancer and played the piano and wore her hair pulled back. His other sister was an artist. She then in detail described both his children. All this information he said was correct. At the time he was engaged and I found out later the he was told not to marry this girl that in 3 months it would be over. The girl he would end up with was described to him. He would marry the other girl and move back to his home town and would work for the county in a high position. They would have 2 children and would eventually move back to Florida. They would in time retire back north in his home town. It is now 2008 and the majority of this had happened. They moved to his home town where he was City Manager. He is currently living in Florida with his new wife, newly born daughter and trying to have that second child. I would have never seen this coming as they both had children and were approaching their 40's. Her readings were not always accurate on time as far as from what I understand there is no time on the other side. However, with my boss her time was very accurate up to the month that he would be leaving to move up north. She once told him she saw him looking over the motor of a boat stuck out in the Gulf. She could see several people gathered around the motor. That night he laughed about it as he was going to look at a boat the next day. Well believe it or not the next day the boat died in the middle of the gulf. As he was gathered around the motor with several other gentlemen it hit him that this is what Tracy said would happen. The Captain made the comment that in 20 years this had never happened to him. These are only a few detailed description that were told to him and happened.

Another co-worker was told that she saw him equal to my boss and that he would be taking his place. He would also be taking about 6 weeks off and visit family. In the near future he would meet a woman, and described her, it would be a short courtship and they would be married. His mom would die before the wedding and they would have 3 children. As he was older they would start their family as soon as possible. At the time he thought she was crazy as he had no desire to take over the position of his current boss and there was no way he would ever be able to take off that much time. Believe it or not, due to various circumstances it all happened. They currently have 1 child working on the 2nd. She also saw, for sometime now, that he would have a gun to his head. She only told him this because she wanted him to know that when it happens he would be o.k. and not to worry. She described the person and it would basically be a disgruntled employee.

This hasn't happened yet but with all the details of his past he is more a believer than not.

Since I have known Tracy I have sent several people to her just to try and prove her wrong. It was just the opposite. I have seen many of my friends get married, get divorced, have children as Tracy told them with great detail about each event. One of my friends was told that her oldest daughter had an abortion and told her why she could not tell her but would find out soon. She was shocked but found out that this had happened. One of my daughter's friends was adopted from overseas. She is now in her 30's and she was told that she would meet her birth mother. A few years ago. That happened. I could write my own book on Tracy but I will leave that to the experts.

She had told several of us about 9-11. When I worked at the airport she told me that we would be shut down for several days in September due to a bomb scare. She knew something horrible was going to happen in New York and she had begged her friends to get out of New York as she knew some would die if they didn't.

As for myself, I've been shocked at what she has told me and what happened. When I first went to Tracy I was divorced. I knew my husband had cheated on me even though I never caught him. It was a girl in his office and I found out later that the entire office wanted so bad to tell me, but couldn't and didn't think I would believe them. Tracy told me, yes, he did cheat on you and without missing a beat described what the girl looked like. She was dead on. She also told me that he would do the same thing to his current wife and they would end up divorced. Since that time I received an e-mail from his wife. She asked me if I knew of a girl that went to high school with me, as my husband and I were high school sweethearts she thought I might know the girl. She had caught him having an affair with her for the past 2 years. They are now divorced and come to find out she never knew he had cheated on me.

I have 2 lovely daughters. My youngest daughter is in the Air Force, married with 3 children. Before she was married Tracy told me that she would have 3 children 2 girls and a boy. That is exactly what they have. My daughter was in the north of Florida taking training as she was going to be deployed to Korea for one year. My daughter had a reading and said "Mom she doesn't know what she's talking about. She didn't even tell me that I was going to Korea." I said "Well I will ask her why." At the time my daughter lived in Colorado. Tracy told me that she would not be going to Korea and she would be pregnant with their 2nd child and that she would be telling me soon. She would also move closer to home. About a month and half later I found out she would move closer to me.

They were then re-stationed in South Carolina.

As for myself, Tracy had told me about a man I would meet and be with for quite a while. This would be a good man and he would be someone I worked with. She told me what he looked like and even a conversation that I would have with him. What a shock this was when it happened and the conversation was almost word for word and I wasn't the one doing the talking.

As for my future, the following has not happened but you can understand if or when it does there will be no misunderstanding that this is a gift that most of us do not nor ever will understand. I am currently working for a great boss before was a horse of a different color and my current boss protected me from him as I had to report him to our HR department, which I won't go into. Tracy has told me that he will be fired and that he will blame me. He will come after me and push me. I will fall down and later be put in the hospital. I will be in the hospital for about 6 weeks as I will have kidney failure from the fall where I hit myself. I am overweight and have been trying to get back into my size 8. She said I will lose about 60 pounds before this happens and that the weight will drop off of me. My friend's husband will die around the same time. My daughter will be deployed overseas and will be called back because the doctor's think I am going to die. My daughter will also get out of the Air Force. During the time she returns to be with me at the hospital she will find out that where she was stationed was bombed and many were killed. My other daughter will be in training for the FBI as there will be another terrorist attack that will make 9-11 look like a picnic. Her background is in forensic science. Once I recover I will sue and receive a substantial amount of money. At this time I will be very happy with my life. Shortly after my recovery my close friend and I will go on a cruise where I will meet a dark haired, blue eyed, dark skinned, well dressed, wealthy man that lives somewhere in Europe. She has told me that this man is my soul mate and that he will come to America to marry me. If this happens you can call me Cinderella!!! Keep in mind that she has told me about this man from my first visit with her in 1999.

Tracy predicted these events many years ago, currently I have been on a diet that is wonderful and yes I have been dropping the weight off around 3 pounds a week. I have currently lost 35 pounds. My daughter is going to be deployed in October of this year. By the end of 2009 she will be getting out of the Air Force. My friends' husband is now under Hospice care and his condition is declining. My old boss, has been investigated several times since I left his office. My oldest daughter has not been called to the FBI, but she will not until the next terrorist attack and when she is I will be in the hospital. Tracy has always told her they would call her around November. This is July and with everything happening as it is. If these things are to happen will be this year.

As we have all been given different gifts, I do not pretend to understand the type of gift that Tracy has received. However, I have come to know Tracy and become a good friend. She takes what she does very serious and I know at times it must be very difficult to see some of the things she sees. It is a gift that carries with it misunderstanding and disbelief as there are many psychics out there that really are not psychics, just as there are doctors and other individuals that should not be doing their craft because they do it poorly.

Delilah

Tracy and I haven known each other since the mid to late 1990's. The first time I ever experienced her gift was when she was on a radio show in Fort Myers Florida. I was blown away with how accurate she seemed to be with the callers! During that time, I was having problems with my marriage and my business so I decided to set up an appointment with her. This was the first time I ever had a psychic reading, and one that was face to face. I have to say, Tracy is compassionate beyond anyone I've ever known, yet helps give you direction! She helps you face life's challenges in a much better light! My first experience with her was totally amazing and it was also the start of a great friendship!!

Throughout the course of our friendship, we have been through so much together!! Things that best friends go through and help each other through. Many times I asked for her help with looking into business decisions...... relationship decisions...... and without fail, she was always right on with what she "saw"!!! I never doubted her!! She has helped me in so many areas of my business with animal related health questions and concerns..... worker concerns..... and what direction I should take. One day out of the blue she called me to say watch out for a worker that will say that I didn't give her the right amount on her check..... So I had a few other workers double check my work and we documented everything about 4 times...... Well, that worker tried to say I didn't pay her right and I had it all documented to show her..... Never heard another word about it. Had I not listened to Tracy's concern, we would have been out a lot of money!

I was lucky enough to try my hand at ghost busting with Tracy. The home owner sent photos to her that had many apparitions in them, that the owner asked Tracy to come check it out! I have always been fascinated by the possibility of seeing a ghost, or something like that. So my adrenaline was running high when we got inside the house. Tracy was going room to room accounting for all the past activities that had gone on in the house, and on that land, before this homeowner bought the house. One room had a goose bumped ridden dark feeling...... At one point she saw a family of four that the husband had murdered and then killed himself. She was trying to get "them" to leave..... I ended up getting shoved forward really hard.... I looked behind me to find no one was there. At that point I bolted for the door going outside! My heart was in my throat! I never went back inside... As Tracy finished up there, I started my car, but remembering that after events like this, Tracy always blows out electrical parts in cars..... So I made her walk about a half a mile, continually asking her if she felt better, shake "it" off so to speak, so she didn't and get in my car and blow out my console!

I was always proud to call Tracy my true best friend, and I was never so proud to call her my best friend like I was when she talked to a group of women, that had gone down a wrong path. These women had been to see so many counselors to help them deal with the fact they ended up having their kids taken away..... Tracy took the time to talk to each one of them, one on one......ALL of the women there had worked through so many issues and had found more closure than anyone would allow them to in the past.

Skipping ahead so many wonderful years together, we were truly the BEST of friends!!! Tracy helped me through so much of life's ups and downs. Don't think I could have made it if it wasn't for our friendship!!! She was like the sister I never had!!!

When my husband passed away in 2005, Tracy and I went on a road trip to take his ashes to where we got married, St. Augustine Florida. Even with all the ghost that consume the most haunted city in America, many trying to get Tracy's attention, it was so good to have her with me... When we got back, I had a reading with her..... It was the most incredible reading I've ever had. Most of the times we were together, I never wanted to have her read me, cause it was all about the friendship, not trying to make it seemed like I was around only for her awesome gift. I think she sometimes looked at it as it was what she does in pretty much every aspect of her life, including with her own work, family and friends! So it was something that she never really tried turning off, even when I tried blocking her out so she couldn't read me.... Everything she saw for my years to come, has and is still completely coming true!!! ALL of it!!! It even started freaking me out on how accurate she has been with this reading that has been going on, as she predicted for me, for years!

Tracy is the type of soul that has such a huge heart!! Always gives all of herself, not only to her family and business, but her friends! I have seen her change someone's life and their outlook by giving them choices if something isn't going in a good direction for them. I've seen some of her clients not take her always non judgmental, and compassionate advise, wishing they had.....

For this letter it's been tough to pick out only a few things out of all the things that we have been through together. So many amazing times, so many trying times....but have always been in each others hearts, thoughts and prayers.... They don't come any better than Tracy....

Love you always, Lauri

I have known Tracy for a number of years and there are many memorable stories. The things she has told me always have a way of working themselves out, albeit in sometimes unexpected ways!

During a reading with Tracy she told me I would have a duck but something would be wrong with its bill. I questioned her intently but she kept telling me that yep, it's a duck but something's wrong with its bill. We moved on from there to discuss other things.

After the reading I started lamenting about the duck. How am I going to take care of a duck? Where am I going to keep it? What do ducks eat? Do they need to be with other ducks? What's wrong with its bill? Ahhhh, maybe I'll find a duck with an injured beak! I'll take it home, get it back to health and there it is, my buddy the duck.

Three weeks later I found myself in possession of a duck. My sister had mailed me a package that contained a wooden duck. Its bill chipped during shipping.

The moral of the story, as Tracy will tell you, is that the angels are never wrong. It's our insistence to take what we're told and force it into what we believe will happen instead of letting go.

After a reading there are times Tracy would talk about the future, upcoming events, etc. A few things she's said; Ben and J Lo would not marry, there will be a black male president before a female president, same sex partners will legally marry, and world disasters will increase and become more intense.

I could go on and on about Tracy's skills, insight, and charming personality however one needs to experience it for themselves. Among other things her accuracy and depth are always surprising. One reading is truly worth a thousand words. But I want to keep this short and sweet, just like Tracy.

You rock!
Love, Your AZ Girl

Future Prophecies

The following are in no particular order. These are predictions. I would like to share with the world.

1. People will be divided between homeopathic and modern medicine. Those with health insurance will promote modern medicine; those without will opt for a more homeopathic solution. In truth, we should strive to come up with a happy medium. Both are needed and there is plenty of room for each discipline.
2. Children will no longer need to attend school. They will learn via the computer, at home, with a virtual teacher.
3. When children are old enough to pursue a career, they will be assigned an apprenticeship to learn their trade.
4. People will work more and more from home not only to save on gas, but to protect one another from spreading illness. This will be good for employers because people will become more productive.
5. People will no longer age past thirty. People who are young will always look thirty, and if you are older than that, you will not age any further.
6. We will have a third World War.
7. I don't see any more presidents after Barack Obama. I wonder if we will get rid of the presidential title in favor of

something else. However, my angels were very clear, we will only have forty-four presidents.

8. There are many more natural disasters to come. These will significantly change the present orientations of the landmasses involved.

9. There will be a monorail system above the clouds that will connect the world. It will resemble a scene from out of *Harry Potter*. People will be sucked from one destination to another, with a vacuum-like energy.

10. There will be computerized machines built into the wall of your home that will dispense any type of beverage you want, from martinis to cappuccinos.

11. We will shift to one world currency, and people will also go back to bartering.

12. There will be a divide between rich and poor. The rich will own their own homes, the poor will either rent or live on the street. The interest rates will go through the roof, making it impossible to have reasonable rents. This will cause multiple families to live together under one roof.

13. The moon will be the new Vegas for the rich.

Like any prediction, it is as always a living reading. The writing is on the wall, but we have the ability to take up the challenge and change what we don't like. In the end, it is up to us what kind of future we will create for our children and ourselves.

You must be the change you wish to see in the world.
—Mahatma Gandhi

In Gratitude

*"By embracing pain, fear, and challenges with
gratitude, I discover the real value and meaning
of my life. I am so grateful to be alive"*
—Dr. Darren Weissman

In case you were wondering, I am still the single mom, working as a psychic. My two daughters and I are extremely close. I have had no contact with Lucien or Constantine for almost ten years.

I am grateful to everyone who has crossed my path and has aided me in getting to this point in my life. I feel that everyone has helped me become the person I am today. For all the experiences in my life, I am truly blessed.

To contact the author for a psychic reading. Please visit her website at Tracyvision.tv

43844887R00116

Made in the USA
Lexington, KY
14 August 2015